A Delightful Treat

30-Day Devotional

BY

Tammy Scott

Interior and Cover Design: Watersprings Media House, LLC.,
www.waterspringsmedia.com

ISBN – 13: 978-0692967690

ISBN -10: 0692967699

This book is dedicated to

Frances Brooks

July 24, 1960–March 3, 2015

Table of Contents

Table of Contents

Introduction

Growing up in church can be one of the most rewarding things or it can be one of the most dangerous things. It is a rewarding thing because you get a solid foundation of Christ. You learn how to live a godly life. It can be dangerous because you can learn church and miss Jesus. You can learn all about who Christ is and never ask Him to be the Lord (Ruler) of your life. You can learn all the facts about Jesus, but miss the relationship.

Well, I grew up in church. I probably attended my first church service when I was six weeks old. My mom and dad lived a Christian life before me and my siblings. They practiced what they preached. I grew up in a home where we had family Bible study every Saturday night. During my childhood years, *Amen* and *227* were the Saturday night shows. Each Saturday night my father would gather our family together. My sisters and I would have to sing a selection. We would then all kneel on our knees as our father prayed. He was not one of those preachers who prayed in the church, but didn't pray in front of his family. After prayer, my dad would read and explain a chapter in the Bible to us. When we became old enough to read, we all would read a certain amount of verses. Bible study would conclude with a memory verse assignment. You can call up me or either of my siblings today and we can quote Hebrews 10:10 KJV which says, by the will we are sanctified through the offering of the body of Jesus Christ once and for all.

I truly appreciated my childhood and my upbringing. Well, I eventually grew up and became a church girl. A Bible character I would use to describe myself would be the rich young ruler in Matthew 19. You know the guy who had kept all those commandments from a youth. That was me. I would often stick out my chest and tell how I didn't drink alcohol, how I didn't party all night at the club, and how I wasn't a loose woman sleeping around. You know, the kind of church girl that would look down on everyone that didn't do it like I did. I am the Christian girl who attended church every Sunday, sang in the choir, taught Sunday school, and worked with the youth and children. I was a perfect little member. A member that could follow moral rules, but my heart was so far from God.

I was doing all those things and had never encountered a true relationship with God. You know, that kind of relationship that makes you say, *Oh how I love thy law it is my mediation all the day (Psalm119:97)*. That relationship that turns your prayers from, 'Lord bless me with this and that' to prayers that say teach me to walk upright.

Lord, teach me to abide in you.
Lord, what does it means to diligently seek you.
Lord, teach me to mediate on your word day and night.

That relationship that made you spend your breaks and time off from work reading God's word, praying, reading books, and listening to You Tube sermons for hours. That relationship in which God Almighty begins to show you how you look in His eyes and make you cry out like Isaiah did in Isaiah chapter 6, *"Woe is me! for I am undone."* That relationship that gives you a desire to want to win souls for Christ, and see souls become saved.

Well, in 2012, I begin to experience that relationship. I experienced true salvation. I thought, there has to be more to salvation then attending church every Sunday, singing in the choir, planning programs and events. I just knew that it was more to this Christian life. I remember Sunday after Sunday my pastor would say read and study your word. I would be in church bobbing my head to those lovely words, but I used to go home and not even open my Bible until the next Sunday at church. My pastor was so generous that he would do responsive reading each Sunday before His message for us non-independent Bible readers, the church people who only read their Bible on Sunday morning, to give us a chance to read the Bible for the week.

In 2012, I developed a daily quiet time. I began reading my Bible every day. I also started obeying what was in the Bible. I then began to neglect TV to read more of God's word, and God started growing me. My attitude changed. I was not easily offended. I began to have compassion for others. He also started revealing biblical principles to me. He started allowing me to make connections with His Word. God's Word changed my life.

This book is for believers who are desiring a closer walk with God. Those believers who are just tired of attending church, but who want a closer walk with God. James 4:8 tells us to, *draw nigh to God, and he will draw nigh to you.* I hope as you read this devotional for the next

30 days that the principles in this book will draw you closer to our savior. Remember the secret of the Lord is with them that fear him (Psalm 23:14).

Lord I'm Available to You

Isaiah 64:8- But now, O LORD, thou art our father; we are the clay, and thou our potter; and we all are the work of thy hand.

When we make appointments, we ask the question, "What dates and times do you have available?" When someone needs us to do something for them we usually check to see if we have any available time. Well as believers, God wants us to be available. Available means able to be used or obtained; at someone's disposal. It means not occupied, free to do something.

God is looking for available, useful believers today. God is looking for those who have surrendered all to His purpose. He is looking for those who continually seek His face, not just on Sundays or occasionally on Wednesday nights. It is up to us to make ourselves available to God. God will use us if we desire to be used.

God can use any available vessel. He used a Jew (*Joseph*- Genesis 37 and 39-50) in a foreign land to preserve His people. He used a trickster (*Tamar*- Genesis 38) to give birth to Perez the lineage of which Jesus Christ our Messiah came through. He used a man with a speech impediment (*Moses*- Exodus 4 and Exodus 14) to save His people from a foreign land. He used a prostitute (*Rahab*- Joshua 2) to protect God's spies. He used a doubter (*Gideon*- Judges 6-8) to win a battle with only 300 men. He used a fisherman (*Peter*- Acts 2) to preach on the day of Pentecost in which 3,000 souls were saved. He used a persecutor (*Paul*- Acts 9) to be an apostle to the Gentiles and to write the majority of the New Testament.

The question is not, "Can God use me?" The question is, "Do I want to be used by God?" In order to be used by God, we must become a vessel God can use. We have to depart from sin and allow God to clean us up and fix us up. God cannot and will not use a vessel that feels it is complete without Him. If we want to be a vessel used by God, we must obey 2 Timothy 2:19b KJV, *Let everyone that nameth the name of Christ depart from iniquity.* Iniquity is sin. If we are naming the name of Jesus, depart (leave, withdraw, quit, exit) from sin.

If we depart from iniquity Timothy tells us in 2 Timothy 2:21 that we shall be a *vessel unto honor, sanctified, and meet for the master's use, and prepared unto every good work.* If we keep ourselves clean, we become available for the Master.

We keep ourselves clean by reading God's Word. John 15:3- *Now ye are clean through the word which I have spoken unto you.* John 17:17 depicts Jesus praying to the Father and he prayed, *"Sanctify them through thy truth: thy word is truth."*

God not only wants a clean vessel, but he wants an empty vessel. He wants a vessel that he can fill up with Him. He doesn't want any of our ideas, motives, or attitudes in the vessel He wants to use. He wants only His attributes in the vessel.

In order for us to bring God an empty vessel we have to practice Hebrews 12:1. We have to lay aside those weights and those sins that will slow down our progress in Christ. As believers, we are striving to get higher and higher in Christ, and if we hold on to a lot of baggage it will slow us down.

Have you ever seen a person on TV or maybe in real life hiking up a mountain? That person does not have a lot of baggage going up the mountain with them. They try to pack as light as they can because they are trying to reach their destination. As believers, we are just like that mountain climber. We must pack light to reach our destination.

We must be a student of the Word. It would be strange for a hospital to hire doctors who hadn't studied medicine, an airplane line to employ pilots who hadn't been trained to fly, a school to hire teachers who have had no schooling, so we cannot expect God to employ those who don't study His Word.

God is looking for applicants who take time to study and learn His will. Isn't it strange that we want God to just settle? The job that God is hiring for is the only job that has eternal benefits, but we want Him to hire unskilled, undertrained employers. Remember God can use anyone, but whoever he uses he wants them to sit at His feet and be trained. God used Peter on the day of Pentecost and 3,000 souls were saved, but Peter sat at Jesus' feet for 3 years learning about Him.

In conclusion, God is looking for available people, but remember being available for God's use will require some sacrifice. Sometimes we have to sacrifice our sleep, food, television, social media, family, hobbies, and etc. to get close to God and become available for His use. Keep James 4:8- on your mind it says, *Draw nigh to God, and he will draw nigh to you.* Remember the closer you are to God the sooner you will be used.

#AVAILABLE FOR HIS USE

The Able God

———

Ephesians 3:20- Now unto him that is able to do exceeding abundantly above all that we ask or think, according to the power that worketh in us

The word able means having the power, skill, means, or opportunity to do something. When I taught school, I taught lessons on the suffix - able. The suffix -able means capable of. Our God is able. That means our God is capable. There is absolutely nothing our God can't do. Jeremiah 32:27 says Behold, I am the LORD, the God of all flesh: is there anything too hard for me?

When you understand that God can, then even the most overwhelming, depressing, and disappointing circumstances become less intimidating. In order to remember God is the able God, always reflect on His word. Reflect on verses like Romans 8:28, *"We know that all things work together for good to them that love God, to them who are called according to His purpose."* This verse lets us know our able God is going to work all things for our good. The key to the things working for our good is we must love God. Loving God is more than just saying Lord I love you. John 14:15 tells us if we love God we will keep His commandments, and if we keep His commandments God keeps His promises.

The able God is able, but there are things we must do as well. Psalm 84:11 let us know that our able *God will not withhold good from them who walk uprightly.*

There are some things that can hinder us from seeing the able God at work. The key hindrance is a lack of faith or unbelief. The Bible tells us in Matthew 13:54-58 that the people in Jesus town missed out in seeing His capability because of their unbelief or lack of faith. We must begin to honestly answer these questions: Do I really believe God can do the impossible? Do I really believe God is able? Do I really believe God can do it for me? We need to give an honest respond, not the response that we think should be given, but do I truly believe. The only thing wrong with doubting is not admitting you doubt.

The father that brought his son to Jesus in Mark 9 told Jesus "Lord, I believe; help my unbelief!" We must begin to pray and ask God to help our unbelief and to pray to God what the disciples requested in Luke 17:5 Lord Increase our faith. Our faith in God increases by reading and studying His word. Romans 10:17 says *faith cometh by hearing and hearing the Word of God.* The more we hear God's word the greater our faith increases. Always make time to read God's word. Don't always read God's word in a hurry or on the run. Set aside time each day to read God's word. Value that time. Make that time precious because the only way we will experience the able God is through faith.

The only way we are going to gain that faith is by learning the word because the word reveals the character of God to us. The more we learn of His character the more confidence we will gain in Him.

In conclusion, always remember God is able. He can do the impossible. Yes, He can do the impossible in your life. Don't just believe God can do the impossible in other people's lives, but believe that He can do it just for you. Remember, He will if we walk upright in Him and if we show him love by keeping His commandments.

#HE'S ABLE

Identity Theft

John 10:10-The thief cometh not, but for to steal, and to kill, and to destroy: I am come that they might have life, and that they might have it more abundantly.

Whenever somebody get pulled over by the police, one of the first things the policeman ask for is their I.D. Many times, when we write a check in the store or use our credit card, the store clerk ask us for our I.D. An I.D. is used to prove a person's identity. Well, my friend, when Satan attacks us, we should be able to pull out our identification card in Christ.

As believers, we should know who we are in Christ. Did you know Satan is aiming to snatch our identity from us? He wants us to be ignorant of who we are in Christ. The reason he wants us to be ignorant is so he can steal our identity. He knows that if we know that Christ is our Father that means he can't attack us our Father created all things. He even created Satan.

Be aware of the tactics Satan will throw your way to steal your identity.

TACTIC 1: Wavered Faith

Satan tries to make us wonder if God is real. Is He who he really says He is? Remember Satan doesn't have a problem with us attending church. He doesn't mind us singing in the choir. He doesn't mind us breaking bad habits. He just doesn't want us to believe that Jesus is God. He doesn't want us to believe that Jesus is the way, the truth, and the life. He doesn't want us to believe that Jesus came that we might have life and that more abundantly.

TACTIC 2: Distractions

Satan tries to make our lives so busy that we make very little time to spend with God. He knows that if we don't read the word we can't know God. 1 John 2:3 says, *"And hereby we do know that we know him, if we keep his commandments."* Satan knows the only way we're going to keep God's commandment is that we have to first learn what they are. He knows the only way we are going to learn them is by studying and reading God's word. He also knows that reading God's word is the only place we will learn our identity in Christ.

TACTIC 3: Bringing up Past failures

Satan wants to keep us condemned. He doesn't want us to accept the fact that God forgives and forgets our sin. He hates when we pull our identification out, and he sees Isaiah 43:25 which says, *"I, even I, am he that blotteth out thy transgressions for mine own sake, and will not remember thy sins."* He hates reading our I.D. which says I am not condemned in Christ (Romans 8:1). He loves to see Christian feeling guilty about sins they have committed in the past. He wants us to be like Joseph's brothers in Genesis 49:15-16. They came up with a scheme because they felt Joseph would abandon or punish them after their father's death. These boys were condemning themselves because of their past. Satan wants to bring up our past because he wants our identity.

TACTIC 4: Discontentment

Paul said in the book of Philippians that he learned to be content. As believers we must learn to be content. Satan tries to remove contentment from our lives, by always showing us other people gifts and talents. We can become so consumed watching other people work their gifts that we forget that God has given us a gift to work. Satan doesn't want us to pull out our I.D. card that says, God has a plan for us (Jeremiah 29:11). He knows that once you realize God has a plan that's just right for you, you won't consume yourself with wishing you had someone else's gifts or talents.

In conclusion, we must remember that we are somebody in Christ. Without Christ, we are nothing. We must always remember who Christ is because the more we think on who He is the more confident we get because we are in Him.

We must always be prepared to show Satan our identification card when he comes to try to steal our identity. Our card will read Child of God who is hidden in Christ (Colossians 3:3), a new creature in Christ (2 Corinthians 5:17), free from the past (Romans 8:1), who is unique (Psalm 139:14), in a relationship with Christ (2 Corinthians

5:18), able to communicate with God (Ephesians 2:18), and a place where Christ dwells (1 Corinthians 3:16).

You Can't Have My Identity

Is God Your Top Priority?

Colossians 3:2- Set your affection on things above, not on things on the earth.

A priority is a thing that is regarded as more important than another. We often hear people say I need to prioritize my day. We all know of people whose lives are already planned out for months. Well, as a Christian, one of the top things in our life should be spending time with God. We must learn to make God a priority just like we make it a priority to eat, brush our teeth, take a bath, watch TV, etc. Before we go on, ask yourself these questions, and give an honest answer. Don't give the answer that you feel a good Christian would give. Be honest. God can't help us until we confess our sins.

1. How much time do you spend each day reading your Bible and praying?
2. How much time do you spend each day watching TV?
3. How much time do you spend each day talking on phone, hanging out, or texting family members and friends?
4. How much time a day do you spend on social media?

5. If you prioritized the following questions which activity on your list get the most time?

If God was *not* the top priority, we must begin to make Him the top. There are so many things in our lives pulling for our attention: spouses, jobs, children, hobbies, family, and friends. We have to make sure that we don't let all these things, which are all good things, become more important than our relationship to Christ. God wants to be our number one priority. **NO EXCEPTIONS!**

We might be wondering how I can fulfil all these duties plus make God number one. The answer is make God number one, and it is His responsibility to make sure you can fulfil all these duties. His word tells us in Matthew 6:33, *"To seek first the kingdom of God, and his righteousness; and all these things shall be added unto us."* Our jobs, health, family, friends, and etc. are all just an add on.

How do I begin to make God the top priority in my life?

1. **Establish a quiet time-** Set up a time in which it is just you and God. A time in which you pray to God and a time in which you read His word. We must stop trying to fit God in our day, but begin to fit our day around God.

2. **Meditate on God's Word throughout the day-** Meditate means to think on. Each day find a scripture, and think on that scripture throughout the day. Since we are living in the technology age, the age in which everyone is always on their phone, send yourself a text of that scripture. Set up your phone, so it can text you the scripture every hour. For those

of us who are still old fashion write the scripture on an index card, put it in your pocket, and pull it out throughout the day. Mediating on God's word yields great results, see Joshua 1:8 and Psalm 1:3.

3. **Draft an accountability partner-** Find a fellow believer that can hold you accountable for your growth in Christ. Remember we are workers together (2 Corinthians 6:1).

In conclusion, let us make sure Christ is a top priority in our life. Let us not forget we can do nothing apart from Christ. Let us remember, if we seek Him first, it is up to him to take care of everything else.

CHRIST IS MY TOP PRIORITY

Caution! Watch Out! Watch the Sign Part 1

2 Timothy 3:1-4 - This know also, that in the last days perilous times shall come. For men shall be lovers of their own selves, covetous, boasters, proud, blasphemers, disobedient to parents, unthankful, unholy, without natural affection, trucebreakers, false accusers, incontinent, fierce, despisers of those that are good, traitors, heady, high minded, lovers of pleasures more than lovers of God.

As drivers, we have different signs on the road. The signs are on the road for us to have safe travels. We see signs like STOP, DEAD END, DETOUR, ONE WAY, etc. On this Christian walk, we have signs in the road to help us have a safe journey. Our road map is the Bible and we must watch out for the caution signs God put right in front of us.

Many of these signs are found in 2 Timothy 3:1-4. As believers, we must make sure that we are avoiding these signs or attitudes people will have in the last days, and we know these are the last days.

Before you continue this devotion, pray and ask God to search your life and to reveal to you anything that is hindering your walk with him.

ATTITUDE #1- **Men shall be lovers of their own selves**.

Stop and make sure you are not self-centered. Make sure that it's not all about me, me, and me. The reason our society is falling apart is because men have become lovers of themselves. Many times, people think drugs, alcohol, and crime is the reason our society is in trouble, but the reason our society is broken down is because people are self-centered.

For example, drug abusers are not thinking about those children they are abandoning for a high. They are not thinking about the people who will have to take care of them once they abuse their body, and fall into bad health. They don't take time to think about how their children and family are suffering because of their abuse. They are just a lover of themselves. As believers, we must make sure we are not just thinking about ourselves and our comfort.

ATTITUDE #2- **Covetous**

Covetous can lead you to a **Dead End.** Covetous is when we have a desire to possess something and usually something that belong to someone else. Colossians 3:5 tells us covetousness is idolatry and in that same chapter Paul teaches us to put it to death. There is nothing wrong with wanting or desiring things, but we shouldn't let our desire of these things cause us to fall into covetousness. Did you know many believers are in debt today because of covetousness?

They saw something that they could not afford, but they wanted it, so they bought it. The sin of covetousness is one we must look out for as a believer. It is so dangerous that when it is carried out it leads to other sins, such as stealing, lying, and even adultery. We can avoid covetousness by setting our focus on obeying God rather than obtaining things.

ATTITUDE #3- Boasters-

Make a quick **U-Turn** when you find yourself boasting. Turn the attention off of you. A boaster is a person who brags on themselves. This is an attitude that can sneak into a believer's life. We should only boast in the Lord. 1 Corinthians 1:31 tells us He that glorieth, let him glory in the Lord. Don't get so excited about your accomplishments that you forget the God who allowed you to accomplish things.

ATTITUDE# 4- Proud- *Cautious!*

Do not let pride set in your life. Pride is when we show oneself above others. Ask yourself these questions: Do I think I am better than others? Am I often putting down others? Do I dwell more on other people's weakness rather than their strengths? The Bible tells us in Philippians 2:3, "…to esteem others better than ourselves." The way I can esteem others better than myself is to become a cheerleader or coach for others. Be the one building up others. Seek out ways to help others utilize their gift. We must always keep in mind that God resists the proud. Let us begin to make people feel encouraged after being around us instead of belittled.

ATTITUDE #5- Blasphemers-*Stop!*

Don't be named among the blasphemers. Blasphemers are people who mock God. People who sit around and make jokes about God, His word, and His people. Many time as believers, we blaspheme God when we laugh at comedians making jokes about the church. We engage in blasphemy of God when we watch shows that belittle and brings down the church. Although, there is nothing wrong with watching TV, we must make sure we are not finding pleasure in things that is making God's name and His people look bad. The church can never be that light to the world if we are engaged in its darkness.

ATTITUDE #6- Disobedience to parents

When we look over our society today, we will see that many children don't have any respect for their parents or authority. The reason is most parents have failed to teach their children. Proverbs 22:6, instructs us to train up a child in the way they should go. The promise behind training them up is that when they are old they will not depart from it. Many parents prevent their children from receiving the blessing God promises them in Ephesians 6:1-3 because they are not teaching them to obey. Parents, allow your child or children to have the opportunity to be blessed. Slow down and teach your children to obey you and all other authority.

In conclusion, these are six attitudes we should be cautious about. Let us make sure these attitudes are not displayed in our lives as a believer. Tomorrow, we will discuss six more attitudes we should be cautious about.

ATTITUDE CHECK

Caution! Watch Out! Watch the Sign Part 2

2 Timothy 3:1-5-This know also, that in the last days perilous times shall come. For men shall be lovers of their own selves, covetous, boasters, proud, blasphemers, disobedient to parents, unthankful, unholy, Without natural affection, trucebreakers, false accusers, incontinent, fierce, despisers of those that are good, Traitors, heady, high minded, lovers of pleasures more than lovers of God;

ATTITUDE # 7-Unthankful!

Stop and give thanks. We all know that a thankful person shows gratitude and appreciation, but we are living in a time when people are just unthankful. Do you find yourself often complaining and rarely ever being grateful? We are living in a time in which people feels that you owe them. If you don't do it for them when they want it and how they want it, they become upset. As believers, let us make sure we do not become unthankful people. The Bible instructs us to give thanks in everything. Let people know we appreciate them no matter how big or small. Let us also make sure we are letting God know we appreciate Him. We can show our appreciation to God through obedience. As believers, let us make sure that every day is a day of thanksgiving, and let us strive to be thankful.

ATTITUDE # 8- Unholy- *U-turn* *to holiness.*

Holy means dedicated or consecrated to God. 1 Peter 1:16 says, *Be ye holy; for I am holy.* I attended a Bible class and the teacher of the Bible class instructed us to read the verse backwards. This is what the verse says backwards, *holy am I for holy ye be.* When I read Isaiah 6, I see the power of the holiness of God. God is so holy that the seraphim's faces are covered as they cried *Holy, holy, holy; is the LORD of hosts: the whole earth is full of his glory.*

Many times, we have in our heads all that we are going to do when we see Jesus; But I am beginning to believe like a close friend of mine says, we are going to be flat like a pancake when we truly see the holiness of God. When we are unholy, we display sinful and wicked ways. A person who is truly saved lives a holy life. Yes, a person can backslide and leave the faith, but the Bible proves to us when a believer is confronted with their sin, repentance takes place immediately.

Our biblical examples are David and Peter. A person who is striving to live holy doesn't make plans to sin and doesn't enjoy sinning. 1 John 1:6 tells us, *"If we say that we have fellowship with him, and walk in darkness, we lie, and do not the truth."* This verse is letting us know that God is not moved by our words. He is moved by our obedience to His Word. Holiness is a trademark of Christ dwelling in us.

ATTITUDE #9- Without natural affection

Watch out for this **Dead-End** attitude. A person who displays this attitude is unloving and unforgiving. They engage in things that are not natural. We have all read articles in the newspaper or heard reports on the news in which people have killed their children, killing their spouses, and many times killing themselves. I recently read a report in which a man killed his two daughters. He called 911 to tell them his daughters were dead. He then shot his wife in the leg and told her that he wants her to live to suffer. He then shot himself. He had no love in his heart. As believers, we must watch out for sins that can lead us to this point. Sins like bitterness and rage. We must make sure we pull those things off like Paul encourages us to do in Ephesians 4.

ATTITUDE #10- Trucebreakers

One who violates a covenant. A trucebreaker is a person who doesn't keep their word or break a promise. This is an attitude that we easily ignore in the church. Many believers made a commitment to the church that they joined, but they rarely attend services. Many believers make commitments to different ministries in the church and they are not faithful to it. An unfaithful person is a trucebreaker. Many faithful believers sit in the church and not realizing they are carrying the trucebreaker attitude. We have made covenants with people saying we will pay this bill each month, but we are failing to pay it. We have gotten so bold that we even ignore the call. We don't make any attempt to let the people know we have fallen into a bind, we know the commitment we made, and to ask them to work with us. No, No, we believers just go on as though we never made the bill. **Stop!** Examine your life and make sure this attitude is not a part of your life.

ATTITUDE #11- False accusers-

A person who brings false charges against someone. Exodus 20:16, tells us not to bear false witness. As believers we should not spread gossip. If you didn't hear it from the source don't spread, it because you could be helping to spread false accusation. When people bring you, he-say/she-say information, don't entertain it because that person could be bringing false accusation to you to destroy unity. Proverbs 16:28 tells us a *whisperer separateth chief friends*. **Watch out** for false accusers, and let us make sure we are not one.

ATTITUDE #12-Incontinent- *lacking self-control.*

As believers we can lack self-control in many areas of our lives. Let's take our tongues as an example. We don't monitor what we are about to say. We just let words roll out of our mouths. We exhibit incontinence as it relates to our diets. We just can't say no to that chocolate or sweet tea. Some experience with incontinence with bad habits like smoking, drinking, ungodly relationships, cursing, gambling, etc. Self-control is one of the fruit of the Spirit. The more we walk in the Spirit, the more God will produce those fruit in our lives. Our cure to conquering lack of self-control is to walk in the Spirit. That means allowing God to guide our life, and this is done by abiding in Him. **Yield** to the Spirit so you can have self-control.

On yesterday we read about six attitudes that we should watch out for as believers, and on today, we discussed six more attitudes. As Christians, let us make sure these attitudes are not rearing their ugly heads in our lives. God wants us to reflect his character not these attitudes that keep Him from shining. Tomorrow, we will discuss the final six attitudes we should watch out for.

BE CAREFUL

Caution! Watch Out! Watch the Sign Part 3

2 Timothy 3:1-5-This know also, that in the last days perilous times shall come. For men shall be lovers of their own selves, covetous, boasters, proud, blasphemers, disobedient to parents, unthankful, unholy, Without natural affection, trucebreakers, false accusers, incontinent, fierce, despisers of those that are good, Traitors, heady, high minded, lovers of pleasures more than lovers of God.

Attitude # 13- Fierce- *Stop!*

Be angry and sin not. Fierce is anger and rage. Ephesians 4:26, tells us to be angry and sin not. This scripture lets us know believers get angry, but in our anger, we shouldn't sin. That verse also tells us to settle our anger before we go to bed. It says don't let the sun go down on your wrath. The reason we need to settle it before rest time is because Satan will turn that anger into bitterness or rage. We can't give Satan any room in our minds. As believers always solve the problem that lead to your anger before the day ends. Sometimes the problem can be solved by you just forgiving the person and letting it go.

ATTITUDE #14- **Despisers of those that are good**

Did you know people can hate you for just living righteous before God? You haven't done anything to them. They just hate your lifestyle. They hate that you are choosing to apply God's word to your life. They hate that you are joyful all the times. They don't realize that they can have that same joy by just walking in the Spirit. As believers, let's not be the one hating another Christian because they are choosing to take God at His word. Just go to God and ask him for forgiveness and say like the father in Mark 9, "Lord help my unbelief." Pray and ask God to help you in those areas you are having a hard time trusting him with.

ATTITUDE #15- **Traitors**

A traitor is one who betrays their friends and family. They are the type of people who smile in your face, but stab you in the back. Anytime you see this attitude popping up in your life, think about Judas Iscariot. Do you want to be on the same list with the person who betrayed Jesus? Judas hung out with Jesus for three and a half years. He saw Jesus work miracles. He saw Jesus heal sick people. He saw Jesus raise people from the dead. Yet, he was part of the crowd, but was working all along to betray his friend. Don't be a traitor be a promoter.

ATTITUDE# 16- **Heady**

This person is intoxicated. They are under the influence. We know there are laws that tell us not to drive intoxicated. People have been killed by drivers that are intoxicated. As believers, God wants us to be cautious of becoming intoxicated. Many believers enjoy a little wine, and occasionally drinking with friends after a long day or week of work. Pay close attention to Proverbs 20:1, *"Wine is a mocker; strong drink is raging: and whosoever is deceived thereby is not wise."*

Proverbs 23:29-32, *"Who hath woe? who hath sorrow? who hath contentions? who hath babbling? who hath wounds without cause? who hath redness of eyes? They that tarry long at the wine; they that go to seek mixed wine. Look not thou upon the wine when it is red, when it giveth his colour in the cup, when it moveth itself aright. At the last it biteth like a serpent, and stingeth like an adder."*

ATTITUDE #17- Lovers of Pleasures

This group pf people get more excited about the pleasure of this world than about God. There is nothing wrong with enjoying life. Remember Jesus came that we might have life and that more abundantly. We just shouldn't put our enjoyment of life over our love for God. *(Revisit Day 4- Is God your top Priority?)*

In conclusion, there are 17 attitudes that we need to watch out for as believers. As believers, we should strive not to allow these attitudes to take control of our life. Let us make sure we don't let these attitudes detour us off God's righteous road.

ATTITUDE CHECK

A Form of God

2 Timothy 3:5- Having a form of godliness, but denying the power thereof: from such turn away.

When I think of a form of God, I think of performance. I think of people who have learn how to be actors on a stage. They have learned how to appear to be a Christian, but never experience the power of God. I know about this topic so well because I was that person that had a form of God. Just knowing all about God, but not knowing him as a person who desires a personal relationship with us. I learned how to say amen, clap my hands, stomp my feet, and lift my hands. I formed into a perfect church member. A person who has a form of God does not change anything about their lifestyle, and the reason is because they can't change it. Your lifestyle doesn't change until you are in Christ.

2 Corinthians 5:17 says, *"If any man be in Christ he/she is a new creature."* Having a form of God doesn't change old ways because old ways can only become new when a person is in Christ. When you have a form of God you set your own standards Proverbs 21:2 tells us, *"Every way of a person seem right in their own eyes…"* A person with a form of godliness can read God's standards and still do the

opposite of them because they trust God to accept them for who they are. They say phrases like "God knows my heart", "Nobody is perfect", "We all fighting our demons", etc. People with a form of God usually justify their character. They make excuses for why they are the way they are.

Today, I encourage you to examine your life. Make sure you don't just have a form of God. I think one of the greatest tragedies in life would be to go to church faithfully, yet never have a true relationship with God. Don't have just a form of God and miss salvation. The saddest words a faithful churchgoer could hear from Jesus is Matthew 7:23, *"I never knew you: depart from me."*

I WANT THE REAL THING

NOT A FORM

Day 9

Expectations

Psalm 62:5 My soul, wait thou only upon God; for my expectation is from him

Expectations are strong beliefs that something will happen. When I taught school, I had high expectations for my students. I did not care what level they were on. I did not care about their previous behavior. I mainly knew what I wanted for them and from them. As I recall my last year of teaching, I remember the principal gave us our rolls. The 3rd grade teachers came over. When they saw my roll, they said, "Mrs. Scott I am going to pray for you." You have a rough class. I allowed those words to marinate in my mind. I became furious and just upset. I pondered *"why would this principal give me all these bad children?"* I felt as if she was just being low down to me. It was just a woe is me attitude.

I remember calling my friend and telling her how low down the principal was. I went to my parents' house crying and upset wondering why I am being mistreated. Guess what? I was lowering my expectation for those children. I was taking the report of others and making that my report. My dad said some words that stood out to me. He said, *"Daniel did not ask God to get him out of that situation."* In my head, I was thinking, "Why did he have to throw Daniel on me?" But that encouraged me, and I begin to think about how this was not the first time I had low students. Actually, I was given low students most of my teaching career. I now realized the difference at that point and from the past classes was I was lowering my expectations. I was building my expectations around everyone else's observations. I had not set a goal for them to meet. Therefore, I had to get my attitude back, walk into that classroom, and make those students rise to my expectations. As believers, have we lost our expectation from God? Are we allowing other people's view to get in the way of us reaching the goal God has aligned for our lives? Are the noise and chatter of other people deterring you from what you know God has told you and showed you?

Do I have low expectation in God?

This is a question we must all ask ourselves. We really have to see if we trust God. Are we just saying we trust God because that's what sounds good? Or do we really absolutely trust God? Am I putting limits on God? Do I have God closed up in a box? Do I really believe God can do exceedingly, abundantly above all that I can ask or think? Do I really believe I can ask God what I will, and he will give it? Do I really believe God? Do I think God compromises His word? Do I want God to comprise His word for me? Do I have low expectations in God? Some ways I can determine if my expectations are low:

Worrying- If you are worrying about something, you have low expectation in God. At some point in our lives we have or will experience worry. We may have worried about our family, finances, jobs, health, ministry, retirement, etc. We must remember when we allow worry to encamp our minds that we have lowered our expectation of God. We have closed our ears to Psalm 46:1, that *"God is our refuge and strength, a very present help in trouble."* When we worry, we forget the words Jesus spoke in Matthew 6:25, *"Therefore I say unto you, take no thought for your life, what ye shall eat or what ye shall drink; nor yet for your body, what ye shall put on. Is not the life more than meat, and the body than raiment?"*

Today ask yourself, "Am I worrying about how something is going to work out?" Am I trusting God or am I worrying? Worry reduces our ability to trust God. In other words, we lower our expectation in God. Worry is a total act of disobedience to God. 1 Peter 5:7, says *"Casting all your care upon him; for he careth for you,"* and in Matthew 11:28, Jesus tells us *"Come unto me, all ye that labour and are heavy laden, and I will give you rest."* When we choose to worry, we are refusing to cast all on Jesus and to bring him our problems. In other words, we are telling him he is incapable of solving our problems.

Unthankful- An unthankful person has low expectations of God. Do you often find yourself complaining? Do you talk more about what is going wrong than what is going right? I often compare things to my job as a teacher because that is what I know. I remember spending many afternoons after school or many times during my breaks complaining to teachers about everything that was going wrong in the school. I talked about how the children didn't want to learn, how there are no consequences for the students, how all the pressure was placed on the teachers. Guess what? Everything I was complaining about was true, but where did complaining take me? And guess what? Most of the people I was complaining to were believers just like me.

We all complain, but we hardly ever prayed together about our problem. It hardly ever crossed our mind to even fast about our problem. We found great joy in complaining about our situation. We were complainers not changers. It is easy to complain because we call it venting. Many times, we must vent, but why do we vent to someone who is in the same storm instead of the one who controls the storm? We must remember that when we find ourselves complaining, we have lowered our expectation in God. We are saying Lord we know that Jeremiah 33:3 says, *"Call on you and you will answer and show us great and mighty things."* We know you said that, but I am going to call on my girlfriend, my mom, my sister, etc. I am calling on them. They are going to answer their phone. I am not going to call you and talk to you about my problem. I would rather complain. Lord, I know your word tells me in 1 Thessalonians 5:18, *"In everything give thanks: for this is the will of God in Christ Jesus concerning you."* I know that you said give you thanks, but Lord I am going to choose to complain.

As believers, we must begin to be changers not complainers. If we see a better way to do something, we should start doing it. Do not just complain about it.

Philippians 4:4, tells us to *rejoice in the Lord always and again I say rejoice.* Remember Paul wrote those words while he was sitting in prison. He had all the reason to complain, but he chooses to rejoice in the Lord. Rejoicing is a choice. We must choose to rejoice. Paul teaches us that our attitude doesn't have to reflect our circumstances. We must be joyful and thankful. In Acts 16, Paul and Silas were beaten and placed in jail. They chose to give God thanks and rejoice. They could have easily complained to God, but they choose to give God thanks. Acts 16:25 said, *"And at midnight Paul and Silas prayed, and sang praises unto God."*

What are you doing at midnight? Midnight is during your hour of crisis. Are you worrying and complaining at midnight or are you praying and singing? Paul and Silas choose to pray and sing, and God sent an earthquake and release everyone that was bound. If we would begin to give God thanks, others around us will begin to be set free, but our expectations of God are too low. We really do not think God can work that same miracle he did for Paul and Silas. We do not think God can do it in 2017, although we will boldly say that Jesus Christ is the same yesterday, today, and forevermore. We will boldly say God doesn't change. Yet, we will not have enough faith to get with the friends we are complaining with and begin to praise and magnify God. We'd rather vent and release our burdens than to give God praise so we can become free and the others around us are free. Paul and Silas' praises even allowed their enemy, the jailer, to be saved and his house.

Holding a grudge- A grudge is resentment resulting from a past insult or injury. Are you holding a grudge against someone? Has someone caused pain to you in the past and you are refusing to let go of it? A grudge is a refusal to forgive. It is easy for us to hold an offence against someone who has wronged us. When we hold a grudge, we have lowered our expectation in God. We don't believe Romans 12:19 when God said vengeance is mine; I will repay. When we hold that grudge, we are saying God you not going to pay them the way I want you to repay them. We want God to repay them with judgement, but God just might repay them in love. Think about Jonah.

Jonah wanted the people of Nineveh to suffer. He wanted God to destroy them. Jonah wanted God's vengeance to be his way, but God do not release vengeance the way we want. He does it His way. Joseph on the other hand accepted God's vengeance God's way. God allowed Joseph to bring nourishment to his brothers. God allowed Joseph to be able to be a provider for his family. Many times, when we say vengeance is God's, in our head we're just thinking God is going to smash our enemies, but God is saying I'm going to allow you to be a blessing to your enemy. I am going to prepare you a table in the presence of your enemy. He did not say your enemies wouldn't be able to eat at the table. When we hold grudges, we do not trust God's word.

Isaiah 54:17 says, *"No weapon formed against me shall prosper."* Many times, we pray to God asking him to contradict His word. We want a trial free life. When the word of God plainly tells us, weapons are going to be formed. He did not say people wouldn't come against us, lie on us, belittle us, etc. He said the weapon wouldn't prosper. He told us in Luke 17:1 that offences will come. He told us that we will be offended, but we want to live an offence free life. He then tells us, woe unto the person who caused the offence. He did not tell us to get even. He said the person who caused the offence would be better off with a stone tied around their neck and that they be cast into the sea. The problem is we want to be the one to tie the stone around their neck, and it will be our pleasure to cast them in the sea. We want to do God's part instead of our part. We must release grudges because grudges lower our expectation of God.

The Israelites had low expectation in God- The children of Israel, God's chosen people, had low expectation in Him. You would think a group of people who saw the mighty hand of God would have expectation in Him. God delivered them out of the Egyptian hands (See Exodus 7-11).

They saw God send the ten plagues. They saw the water turn into blood. They saw the plague of the frogs, lice, and flies take over the land. They saw the death of the Egyptian's cattle. They saw the people stricken with boils. They saw the hail and fire God sent. They saw the locust take over the land. They saw God cover the land with darkness. They saw all Egyptian firstborns killed.

Can you believe before they got to the Red Sea they had already lost their expectation in God? In Exodus 14:10-12- *"And when Pharaoh drew nigh, the children of Israel lifted up their eyes, and, behold, the Egyptians marched after them; and they were sore afraid: and the children of Israel cried out unto the Lord. And they said unto Moses, Because there were no graves in Egypt, hast thou taken us away to die in the wilderness?*

Wherefore hast thou dealt thus with us, to carry us forth out of Egypt? Is not this the word that we did tell thee in Egypt, saying, let us alone, that we may serve the Egyptians? For it had been better for us to serve the Egyptians, than that we should die in the wilderness." God had already shown them 10 plagues and yet their expectation was low in God. God did not punish them for having low expectations, but he opened up the Red Sea. Three days later, the Israelites lowered their expectation in God again in Exodus 15:22-27.

They came to a place where they first could not find water, but then they found water and the water was bitter. Instead of them having expectation in God and recalling the miracles God had performed, they chose to murmur instead of having expectation in the God who had turned water into blood and the God who parted a sea for them to walk across.

David had high expectation in God- In 1 Samuel 17, David trusted God to deliver Israel from Goliath and the Philistines. David did not look at His statue. He did not look at his ability. He noticed that Goliath was not circumcised, and he was determined that he would not let this uncircumcised giant defile the army of God. He looked at God's ability and he said to Saul, in 1 Samuel 17:37, *"Moreover, The LORD that delivered me out of the paw of the lion, and out of the paw of the bear, he will deliver me out of the hand of this Philistine."*

He then told Goliath, in 1 Samuel 17:45, Then said David to the Philistine, *Thou comest to me with a sword, and with a spear, and with a shield: but I come to thee in the name of the LORD of hosts, the God of the armies of Israel, whom thou hast defied.* David had confidence that God would deliver. His expectation was in God.

How can I keep my expectation high in God?

Always remind yourself of God's character? Remember who God is. He is Jehovah Jireh, our provider. He is Jehovah Shalom, our peace. He is El Shaddai, the Almighty God. He is our Shepherd, and our strong tower. He is our advocate. He is Holy. He is the all-knowing God. Always keep in mind the awesomeness of our God. For more info on this topic see Tony Evans Book the Power of God's Name.

Read God's Word- The word of God is where we learn the character of God. His word is how our faith is built. The bible tells us in Romans 10:17 faith cometh by hearing, and hearing by the word of God. This verse lets us know that the word of God increases our faith, and the more faith we have in God, the stronger our confident is. Reading the word of God should be a daily part of our life.

We must begin to pray prayers like Psalm 119:18, *Open thou mine eyes, that I may behold wondrous things out of thy law.*

Psalm 119:16, *"Lord help us to delight in your statue and Lord do not let us forget your word."*

Psalm 119:33, *"Teach me, O LORD the way of thy statues; and I shall keep it unto the end."*

Psalm 119:34, *"Give me understanding and I shall keep thy law,* Psalm 119:36 *incline my heart unto thy testimonies, and not to covetousness."*

Psalm 119:38 *stablish thy word unto thy servant."*

We should have a desire to meditate on God's word day and night. He said if we do that we will be like a tree planted by rivers of water that bring forth it fruit and its season. God's word will make us stable, and a stable person is not a wavering person.

The more we read God's word, the more we will crave it, and our testimonies will become like Psalm 119:47- and *I will delight myself in thy commandments, which I have loved,* Psalm 119: 57- *Thou art my portion, O LORD; I have said that I would keep thy law,* Psalm 119:97- *O how I love thy law! It is my meditation all the day,* and Psalm 119:162- *I rejoice at thy word, as one that findeth great spoil.* I remember the promise God left us in Psalm 119:165. He said, *"Great peace have they which love thy law: and nothing shall offend them."*

Seek God- When you are seeking for something that means you are looking for it. Jesus told us in Matthew 6:33 *to seek first the kingdom of God and His righteousness and all these things shall be added unto us.* God is telling us to strive to have an intimate relationship with Him. Let Him become the top priority in our lives. As long as God is our top priority, our expectation will be him. We lower our expectation of God when we take our eyes off him.

James 4:8 tells us to *draw nigh to God and he will draw nigh to us.* The word of God also tells us in Jeremiah 29:13, *And ye shall seek me, and find me, when ye shall search for me with all your heart.*

God confirms this word in Matthew 7:7, *"Ask, and it shall be given you; seek, and ye shall find; knock, and it shall be opened unto you. If we seek God, everything else is an add on."* Those things that cause us to lower our expectation will be eliminated from our life if all our attention was on seeking God. Seeking God is all about doing the work of the ministry. Christ's goal was to please the Father and to serve others. That should be the same goal we as believers should have. Are you doing the work that Christ did?

In Conclusion, let us make Psalm 62:5 our testimony my soul, wait thou only upon God; for my expectation is from him. Let us make our hope in Christ. Colossians 1:27 lets us know that Jesus is our Hope of Glory. Our expectation should always remain high in God because he is the author and finisher of our faith. When He starts a job, He will complete the job. 1 Thessalonians 5:24 says, *"Faithful is he that calleth you, who also will do it."* God is faithful to do what he calls you to do. What vision has God shown you? What dream are you anticipating God to manifest in your life?

Today, I encourage you to trust Him no matter how rocky the road gets, no matter how dark it may seem at times. Do not belittle the promise God has given you. Do not despise the small beginning. Rejoice at the small.

The Bible tells us in Zechariah 4:10 that God rejoice at them beginning the work. He was joyful that they started doing measurements. Work your dream. Trust God for the outcome. Always know if you are doing what God has told you to do, it is His responsibility to see you to see you through.

Remember Hebrews 10:23 says *Let us hold fast the profession of our faith without wavering; (for he is faithful that promised).*

MY EXPECTATIONS ARE IN YOU

Day 10

The Blessed Person

❦

Psalm 1:1-3- Blessed is the man that walketh not in the counsel of the ungodly, nor standeth in the way of sinners, nor sitteth in the seat of the scornful. But his delight is in the law of the Lord; and in his law doth he meditate day and night. And he shall be like a tree planted by the rivers of water, that bringeth forth his fruit in his season; his leaf also shall not wither; and whatsoever he doeth shall prosper.

Psalm 1 is one of my favorite chapters in the Bible. These scriptures are my goal. I want to be that blessed person. What does it mean to be blessed? To be blessed means to have divine favor. Favor is an act of kindness beyond what is due or usual. Psalm 1:1-2 tells us how to be blessed from God. In order to be blessed we have to watch where we walk, stand, and sit. We have to delight in God's law and meditate on his law, day and night. What does all that mean?

DO NOT WALK IN THE COUNSEL OF THE UNGODLY. As a believer, I shouldn't get my advice from ungodly people. In life, people will always be around to give advice. We all know advice can come from friends or family, but advice also can come from magazines, talk shows, movies, songs, and etc. Some advice is good and some is bad, but as a believer we must be careful who we are getting advice from.

There is nothing wrong with seeking counsel. The Bible encourages us to seek counsel. Proverbs 15:22 NLT says, plans go wrong for lack of advice; many counselors bring success. We just have to be sure that the counsel we are seeking is godly counsel. Make sure the advice people gives you lines up with God's word. The way to ensure you don't walk in the counsel of the ungodly is to make sure you are acknowledging God in all your ways.

DO NOT STAND IN THE WAY OF SINNERS. Who am I hanging with? As a believer, I have to watch my company. Standing in the way of sinners means I am participating in their ways and their activities. I must remember in life there are two roads according to Matthew 7:13-14. There is a broad road that leads to destruction and there is a narrow way that leads to life. I have decided to be in the company of people who are choosing the narrow road. How can I determine if my company is walking on the broad or narrow road? We can determine the road by watching the fruit that is produced from the people we hang with. If they are producing fruit of the flesh mentioned in Galatians 5:19-21, they are walking on the broad road. If they are producing fruit mentioned in Galatians 5:22-23, they are walking on the narrow road. To ensure you are not standing in the way of the sinner, constantly ask God to develop you into Psalm 19:14, in which it reads let the words of your mouth and the meditation of your heart will be acceptable in His sight.

DO NOT SIT IN THE SEAT OF THE SCORNFUL. Who is a scornful person? A scornful person is a person sitting around belittling God and His people. A scornful person finds enjoyment in criticizing the people of God and the things of God. As believers, we must be very mindful of making sure we are not participating in things that are bringing down the name and character of God. We have to make sure we are not taking pleasure in things bringing down God's church and His people.

DELIGHT IN THE LAW OF GOD. As believers, we should delight in God's law. Delight means to take pleasure in and find great joy. As believers, we should be excited about God's word because God's word gives us direction. Psalm 119:130 tells us the entrance of thy word giveth light; it giveth understanding to the simple. God's word is pure. It is free of contamination. His word is unlike our words. Sometimes we can exaggerate our words or soften down our words, but God's word is pure. God's word will also stand forever. In Matthew 24:35, the Word tells us heaven and earth shall pass away, but God's word will not pass away.

MEDITATE ON HIS WORD. Meditate means to think about or to be focused on. A blessed person always has God on their mind. A blessed person does not just hear God's word, but they ponder on it or think on it. A person who meditates on God's word allows God to guide their decisions. The only way one can meditate on God's word is by reading and learning it.

In conclusion, if you choose not to walk in the counsel of the ungodly, stand in the way of sinners, or sit down with scornful, but you choose to delight in God's law and to meditate on his law, day and night your result will be a blessed life. Psalm 1:3 says the person who does these things will be like a tree planted by the rivers of water, that bringeth forth his fruit in his season; his leaf shall not wither; and whatsoever he doeth shall prosper.

I AM BLESSED

Day 11
The Lord is my Shepherd

Psalm 23:1- The Lord is my Shepherd I shall not want.

This probably was one of the first verses I learned as a child. This is a very popular verse, most believers can quote this verse, and this is one of the few verses we quote that we know exactly where it is found in the Bible. Do we really know what it means for God to be our Shepherd? Do we really know what position that puts us in?

A Shepherd is a person who tends and rears sheep. This means if God is my Shepherd, I am a sheep. Did you know sheep are not very smart animals? A sheep is in desperate need of a Shepherd. I was reading a book by Dr. Tony Evans once. In his book, he pointed out that we see all types of animals trained in a circus but we have never, ever seen a trained sheep. That phrase really stood out to me because I was able to truly see how much I need Christ.

As a sheep, I am dependent on my Shepherd. Many times, we read Psalm 23:1 trying to receive thee "I shall not want" blessing, but the only way we can walk into the "I shall not want" is to allow the Lord to be our Shepherd. We have to humble ourselves enough to follow the lead of our Lord. Once we truly make God our Shepherd there are vast benefits we will receive.

BENEFIT 1- WE SHALL NOT WANT. Psalm 84:11 let us know he won't withhold any good thing from us if we walk upright. When we make God our Shepherd, we can't help but to walk upright. The only direction we are walking in is the direction He leads us in. God is righteous so he can only walk in righteousness.

BENEFIT 2- HE MAKES US REST. Did you know a believer could be a workaholic? You can find yourself always busy. Trying to meet this goal or that deadline. When we allow the Lord to be our Shepherd he stops and makes us rest. We must remember that our LORD even rested (Genesis 2:2).

BENEFIT 3- HE LEADS US. Our Shepherd directs us. That is why Proverbs 3:6 tell us in all our ways to acknowledge Him. God guides our direction as long as we allow Him to be the Shepherd of our life. Many of the bad decisions we have made in our life happened during times in which we took the role of the Shepherd instead of remaining the sheep. The only way he can lead us into righteousness is that we must chose to follow. That is why the Psalmist in Psalm 119:133 asked God to order his steps. We must remember all of God's directions are found in His Word.

BENEFIT 4- HE RESTORES US. Many times, as sheep we stray from our Shepherd. We go our way and do things the way we want to, but our Shepherd is so loving and merciful that he restores us. He brings us back. He revives us. He restores us through forgiveness. In order to receive that restoration, we come back to him and confess our sins. John 1:9 says he will forgive us our sin and cleanse us from all unrighteousness.

BENEFIT 5- HE IS WITH US. No matter what situation or circumstance we face we must remember our Shepherd is with us. He does not want us to stop and get depressed when problems and disappointments occur in our life. He wants us to keep walking because he is right there with us. Hebrews 13:5, lets us know that our Lord will not leave us. In Daniel 3, the three Hebrew boys faced a situation. They were thrown into a fiery furnace because they refused to bow down to a golden image. When they were placed in the fire God was right there walking in the fire with them.

BENEFIT 6- HE PROTECTS AND COMFORT US. The rod for a Shepherd was a weapon to provide protection. When those wild animals tried to attack the sheep, the Shepherd had his rod there to protect them. Our Shepherd protects us from the enemy and all his tactics. As long as we allow the LORD to be our Shepherd, we don't have to fear.

BENEFIT 7- HE CORRECTS US. A staff was used to correct the sheep when they got out of line. God corrects his children when we get out of line. Hebrews 12:6 (NIV) let us know God disciplines those He loves. According to Hebrews 12:10 he disciplines us so we can share in his holiness. It is not an enjoyment to be corrected or disciplined by God, but this discipline is a sign of the great love He has for us.

BENEFIT 8- HE SHOWCASES US IN THE FRONT OF OUR ENEMIES. Our Shepherd defends and fight for us. The only thing we have to do is remain obedient sheep. His word tells us in Isaiah 54:17, no weapons form against us shall not prosper. He also tells us in Romans 12:19

that vengeance is his. If we remain obedient sheep, God will prepare a table right in the presence of our enemies.

BENEFIT 9- YOUR CUP WILL RUN OVER. God meets our need. Philippians 4:19, says my God shall supply all my need. As long as God is my Shepherd, my needs are met. Many times, we try to take the role of the Shepherd and try to meet our own needs. God is saying let me be your Shepherd and I will meet your needs.

BENEFIT 10- LIVE WITH CHRIST FOREVER- Our ultimate goal as a believer is to one-day dwell with Christ. We want to one day live in that mansion he has prepared for us.

In conclusion, is the Lord your Shepherd? Jesus says in John 10:27, *My sheep hear my voice, and I know them, and they follow me.* Our daily prayer should be Lord make me an obedient sheep.

#THE LORD IS MY SHEPHERD

Expressing Love God's Way

John 13:35- By this shall all men know that you are my disciples, if you have love one to another

Do you know how to truly love God's way? Do we really have genuine love for others? It is easy to say I love you, but it takes work and action to really demonstrate love. God did not *just* say I love you to the world, but he gave His only begotten Son. Romans 5:8, tells us that Christ demonstrated His love for us even while we were yet sinners. Love=Action. 1 Corinthians 13 is the chapter in the Bible that describe true love. What are the characteristics of true love?

CHARACTERISTIC 1- **True love is patient**. Are you patient? Do people get on your nerves really quick? Are you a complainer? Do you worry when things don't happen right away? Patience means being able to accept delays, problems, or suffering without becoming annoyed or anxious. As believers, we must learn patience. We must learn to rest in God instead of complaining to God. We have to wait patiently on God.

CHARACTERISTIC 2- **True love is kind**- Am I really kind? Kind means to be considerate and helpful. It means to be nice. Do people consider you to be a kind person? How do your friends and family see you? If they were asked to describe you, would kindness even enter their mind? When people speak about you do they say phrases like you don't want to rub them the wrong way? Are you that easy to talk to person or are you the person everyone is trying to avoid or get away from? Remember love is kind. We have to begin to develop a kind personality. We cannot base our kindness on how others treat us, but we have to base it on expressing love the way Christ demands. Many times, people associate being kind with weakness. Kindness doesn't mean you allow people to run over you or take advantage of you. This is why we have to acknowledge God in all our ways so He can direct our path in every situation we face.

CHARACTERISTIC 3- **True love is not jealous**. Jealousy is when you resent a person because of their success or advantage. Do you hate to see others succeed? Are you wishing badly on others? We must learn to be content with what and where God has us. We can overcome jealousy by remembering who we are in Christ. Who am I in Christ?

You are created in God's image. Genesis 1:27- *So God created man in his own image, in the image of God created he him; male and female created he them.*

You are unique. Psalm 139:14- *I will praise thee; for I am fearfully and wonderfully made.*

God has a plan just for you. Jeremiah 29:11- *For I know the plans I have for you, declares the Lord, plans to prosper you and not to harm you. Plans to give you a hope and a future.*

Remember, you won't have any time to be jealous if you spend your life seeking and working the plan God design just for you.

You are loved. John 3:16- *For God so loved the world that he gave his only begotten Son, that whosoever believeth in him should not perish, but have everlasting life.*

I have an opportunity to receive wisdom. James 1:5- *If any of you lack wisdom, let him ask of God that giveth to all men liberally, and upbraideth not.*

CHARACTERISTIC 4- True love is not boastful or proud. A proud or a boastful person shows pride and satisfaction in one's achievement. Is it all about you? Are you giving God the credit for your success or are you taking the credit? The key to dealing with pride and boastfulness is to become an encourager. 1 Thessalonians 5:11 tells us to edify others. Philippians 2:3 tells us to esteem others better than ourselves. Always keep in mind how God views a prideful person. James 4:6 tells us God resist the proud. A person who is expressing love God's way is humble. Joyce Meyer listed characteristics of a humble person. Some of the characteristics she listed were:

- A humble person can always ask for help, and doesn't insist on everything being done their way.
- They are quick to forgive
- A peacemaker
- Serve others
- Quick to repent
- Treat others with respect

- Knows when to be quiet

CHARACTERISTIC 5- Love is not rude and selfish- A rude person is an impolite person, and a selfish person lacks consideration for others. A rude and selfish person is only concerned with their happiness. They rarely consider the happiness of others. They do not ever make themselves uncomfortable for others to be comfortable. The key to dealing with being rude and selfish is to become generous. Become a giver. Stop seeking what you can get, but begin seeking ways to help others. You can give of your time, resources, and talents. We can practice this each day by being determined to do something for someone else. Some examples are we can pray for someone else, send an encouraging word to someone, be a listening ear for someone, etc.

CHARACTERISTIC 6- Love doesn't keep a record of wrong. Love is forgiving. It is so easy for us always to bring up past hurts and failures. I often read quotes and phrases that say something to this extent: *You can do 1,000 good things, but the one bad thing you do will cancel out all the good you have done.* When we love God's way that phrase is not true in our lives. Are you often bringing up people's past mistakes? Do you have a problem forgiving others? How would you feel if Jesus always brought up your past? Are you willing to protect someone else's reputation? Love covers. So often we say we love someone, but the minute that person rubs us the wrong way or makes us upset, we begin to sound off the list of all their past faults. Is that really love? We hurt God often, but God never brings back up our past failures. Isaiah 43:25 says he does not even remember our sin. As believers, we must began to let the past stay in the past.

CHARACTERISTIC 7- Love remains faithful. No matter what situation comes in our lives. Love remains faithful. Love does not change on conditions.

In conclusion, as believers we should learn to express love God's way. God expresses love to us by giving of Himself. He was not selfish or full of pride. He did not mind identifying with His creation to demonstrate love to us. He cannot help but love, 1 John 4:8 tells us *"God is love."*

#LORD TEACH ME TO LOVE

Day 13

Our Opponent

1 Peter 5:8 (NLT)– Stay alert! Watch out for your great enemy, the devil. He prowls around like a roaring lion, looking for someone to devour.

An opponent is someone who competes against or fights another in a contest, game, or argument. Most times when people have an opponent, they try to learn as much as they can about that opponent. Basketball players and football players spends hours not just practicing, but watching footage of their opponent. They trying to learn their opponent's strengths and weaknesses.

Well, as believers, we must learn about our opponent. Our opponent is Satan, and we are fighting against him every day. This is not an opponent who we will see once or twice in a season. This opponent is ready to battle every single day, and he is ready to battle from the time we wake up until we go to bed. Sometimes, he even tries to fight us in our dreams. So, exactly what do we need to know about this opponent?

The first thing we need to know about this opponent is his character. This opponent is the total opposite of God. God is **truth**. In John 14:6, Jesus says *"I am the way, the truth, and the life."* This opponent is a **liar**. 2 Corinthians 11:14- *"But I am not surprised! Even Satan disguises himself as an angel of light,"* and John 8:44 let us know he is a liar and the Father of lies.

God is a **giver**. John 3:16- *"For God so loved the world that he gave His only begotten Son."*

This opponent is a **thief**. John 10:10 says, *"The thief cometh not, but for to steal, and to kill, and to destroy."* Satan wants to steal every blessing from us that God wants to give us. In the book of Daniel, he held up Daniel's blessing for 21 days.

God is **light**. 1 John 1:5- *"This then is the message which we have heard of him, and declare unto you, that God is light, and in him is no darkness at all."*

This opponent **blinds**. 2 Corinthians 4:3-4, *"And even if our gospel is veiled, it is veiled to those who are perishing. The god of this age has blinded the minds of unbelievers so that they cannot see the light of the gospel that displays the glory of Christ, who is the image of God."*

God is a **friend**. John 15:15, *"Henceforth I call you not servants; for the servant knoweth not what his lord doeth: but I have called you friends; for all things that I have heard of my Father I have made known unto you."*

This opponent is an **enemy**. 1 **Peter 5:8**, *"Be alert and of sober mind. Your enemy, the devil, prowls around like a roaring lion looking for someone to devour."*

The next thing we need to know is this opponent is the weakest opponent because he only has three ways to fight. He has been fighting in these ways since he began his fight. The three ways he can fight is found in 1 John 2:16, *"For all that is in the world, the **lust of the flesh**, and the **lust of the eyes**, and the **pride of life**, is not of the Father but is of the world."*

Lust of flesh- gratifying physical desires

Lust of eyes- is a desire to possess what we see

Pride of life- self-exalting

Every sin that anyone has committed or will ever commit will fall under one of these categories. The story of Adam and Eve is a biblical example:

Genesis 3:6- *"And when the woman saw that the tree was good for food, and that it was pleasant to the eyes, and a tree to be desired to make one wise, she took of the fruit thereof, and did eat, and gave also unto her husband with her; and he did eat."*

Lust of the flesh- tree was good for food

Lust of eyes-it was pleasant to the eyes

Pride of life- tree to be desired to make one wise

Satan already knows he has lost the battle. He trying to keep us distracted so that we will give up in the midst of the game. Satan thought he won the victory when he deceived man, but Jesus confirmed Satan lost when he shed His blood on Calvary, because of Jesus death, burial, and resurrection we are:

Conquerors- Romans 8:37- *"Nay, in all these things we are more than conquerors through him that loved us."*

Overcomers- 1 John 5:5- *"Who is he that overcometh the world, but he that believeth that Jesus is the Son of God?"* 1 John 4:4- "Ye are of God, little children, and have overcome them: because greater is he that is in you, than he that is in the world." Revelation 12:11, *"And they overcame him by the blood of the Lamb, and by the word of their testimony; and they loved not their lives unto the death."*

Victorious- 1 Corinthians 15:57, *"But thanks be to God, which giveth us the victory through our Lord Jesus Christ."*

In conclusion, the devil is a manipulating, deceiving, and cunning opponent, but as a believer we can have victory over him. We have victory because of Jesus who died on the cross for our sins. We must remember Satan is a weak opponent. He doesn't have any new tricks just new candidates. As believers, let us stay prepared so that we won't be a candidate for Satan's tricks.

#Satan is not a team player, He is my opponent

Am I Wise or Am I Foolish

James 1:5- If any of you lack wisdom, let him ask of God, that giveth to all men liberally, and upbraideth not; and it shall be given him.

I n life we have to make decisions. The decisions we make are either wise or foolish. **Who gives wisdom?** Proverbs 2:6 for **the Lord** giveth wisdom: out of his mouth cometh knowledge and understanding.

How do we obtain wisdom? Proverbs 1:7 the **fear of the LORD** is the beginning of knowledge: but fools despise wisdom and instruction.

How valuable is wisdom? Proverbs 16:16 how much **better** is it to get wisdom **than gold**! And to get understanding rather to be **chosen than silver**!

Wisdom is having or showing experience, knowledge, and good judgment. Did you know that many people can have a lot of knowledge and a lot of experience and still be foolish? What is being foolish? Foolish means lacking good sense or judgement.

How can we tell if you are wise or foolish?

Proverbs 10:21, NLT "*The godly gives good advice, but fools are always destroyed by their lack of common sense.*" In this verse, the wise is giving good advice, and fools are being destroyed. We must ask ourselves the question: *What do I do when I am given good advice?* Every Sunday our pastors are standing over the pulpits giving us good advice. Are we listening to and following the advice or are we closing our ears to the advice? If we listen to the advice, we will become advisors. That means we will start giving advice. If we don't listen to the advice, we will be destroyed. Remember Hosea 4:6- "*My people are destroyed for lack of knowledge: because thou hast rejected knowledge.*"

Proverbs 10:23, NLT "*Doing wrong is fun for a fool, while wise conduct is a pleasure to the wise.*" This verse is letting us know, the foolish love to do wrong. They enjoy participating in those things that displease God.

Proverbs 16:16, "*How much better it is to get wisdom than gold! And to get understanding rather to be chosen than silver!*" A wise person values wisdom over riches. Yes, it is nice to have money, but wisdom can take you farther. A wise person can obtain riches and know exactly what to do with it. They know how to invest it, save it, and give it. A foolish person obtains riches and the only thing they know how to do with it is waste it and spend it. A foolish person rarely gives it. An example is the prodigal son in Luke 15. The son went and asked his father for his portion. A few days after asking the son went on his journey. Verse 13 of Luke 13 says, he wasted his substance with riotous living. The young son spent everything, and when everything was spent a famine arose in the land and the young son was now not spending but begging.

Remember, a wise person wants wisdom over riches because the wisdom will instruct you on how to prepare for the future.

Check out how Joseph used wisdom in Genesis 41. The pharaoh had a dream. Joseph interpreted his dream. He said there's going to be seven years of plenty and seven years of famine. Joseph told the pharaoh to store up food during the year of plenty, so when the year of famine came they would have food. Wisdom instructed Joseph how to prepare for the future.

Proverbs 23:9, NLT- *"Don't waste your breath on fools, for they will despise the wisest advice."* A foolish person ignores good advice. An example is Saul. Saul kept disobeying God even after rebuke. In 1 Samuel 13 Saul disobeyed God by burning a sacrifice to God. Saul should have never burned a sacrifice to God because he was not a priest. In verse 13 of 1 Samuel, Samuel told Saul, *"thou hast done foolishly: thou hast not kept the commandment of the Lord thy God, which he commanded thee: for now, would the Lord have established thy kingdom upon Israel forever.* In verse 14, Samuel told Saul, *"But now thy kingdom shall not continue: the Lord hath sought him a man after his own heart, and the LORD hath commanded him to be captain over his people because thy has not kept that which the Lord commanded thee."* Instead of Saul letting this rebuke change him a few chapters later he disobeyed God again in 1 Samuel 15. God told Samuel to smite the Amalek. He told him to destroy all that they have. Saul decided to keep the King. Saul and the people also spared the best of the sheep, and of the oxen, and all that was good. God said destroy all. Saul and the people said we are keeping the best.

Proverbs 24:5, *"A wise man is mightier than a strong man, and a man of knowledge is more powerful than a strong man."* Strength without a plan is a disaster. You can have all the power but if you don't have wisdom and knowledge your power is weak. In the natural body, eating properly and exercising will help us gain our strength. How do we develop spiritual strength? We develop physical strength by reading our Bible, listening to God's word, meditating on God's word, fellowshipping with other believers, and praying. If we do these things, we will increase in God's wisdom and knowledge. In Colossians 1:9 Paul prayed for the Colossian believers. He prayed that they might be filled with the knowledge of his will in all wisdom and spiritual understanding. This is a prayer all believers should pray for one another.

Matthew 7:24-25, *"Therefore whosoever heareth these sayings of mine, and doeth them, I will liken him unto a wise man, which built his house upon a rock: And the rain descended, and the floods came, and the winds blew, and beat upon that house; and it fell not: for it was founded upon a rock."* A wise person hears God's word and react or respond to it. When the storm of life begins to rage and when it seems like everything is falling apart, the person who heard God saying and reacted to it can stand on the word of God in times of trouble. We have to read God's word, meditate on it, and study it in order to build a solid foundation.

In conclusion, let us strive to be wise. Remember, God is the one who gives wisdom, and he gives it generously. He just wants us to ask Him. Remember, He is the only wise God our savior.

I AM WISE

The Things God Hate

Proverbs 6:16-19, These six things doth the Lord hate: yea, seven are an abomination unto him: A proud look, a lying tongue, hands that shed innocent blood, an heart that deviseth wicked imaginations, feet that be swift in running to mischief, a false witness that speaketh lies, and he that soweth discord among the brethren.

As believers, we are in a relationship with Christ. Anytime we get in a relationship with someone we want to learn their likes and dislikes. I wonder why the most important relationship we will ever have we don't take time out to find out what God hates. We enjoy talking about God's love, His mercy, His peace, etc., but we spend very little time learning about the things God hate.

Proverbs 6:16-19 list those things God hate:

1. **A proud look**- A proud look is when one is looking down on another. A prideful person sometimes doesn't realize they are full of pride. They sometimes mistake it for having high self-esteem or not being a push over. A prideful person's end destination is a fall. Proverbs 16:18, tells us pride goeth before a fall. James 4:6, lets us know that pride is something that God resist.

How to deal with a proud look. Deal with pride by following Romans 12:3 to not think of ourselves higher than we ought. We also should practice Philippians 2:3 to esteem others better than ourselves.

2. **A lying tongue-** A person who speak falsely with intention to deceive. Proverbs 12:22, tells us lying lips are abomination to the LORD. We must remember that lying lips make us resemble Satan's character. Remember he is a lie and the father of lies.

How to deal with a lying tongue- You deal with a lying tongue by being honest. Follow Colossians 3:9, which says lie not one to another, seeing that ye have put off the old man with his deeds;

3. **Hands that shed innocent blood-** destroying someone's body or spirit. Many times, we just think of murder when we talk about shedding innocent blood, but when we hate someone and make no room in our hearts to forgive, it is like we are committing murder. 1 John 3:15 says whosoever hateth his brother is a murderer. Do you know many people commit murder with their tongue? They kill and destroy people's reputations, integrity, and names with that little member, the tongue. Remember, Proverbs 18:21, says death and life are in the power of the tongue.

How to deal with hands that shed innocent blood. You deal with hands that shed innocent blood by practicing forgiveness. We must always be open to forgive. In Mark 18, when Peter asked Jesus how many times he should forgive someone who sin against him. Jesus replied seventy times seven. Ephesians 4:32, tells us to forgive one another just like Christ forgave us.

4. **Heart that deviseth wicked imaginations** is a heart that plots evil. A person who make plans to sin. Proverbs 4:16 NLT tells us that evil people cannot sleep until they have done their evil deed for the day. Some people have made it a habit to sin. It is like they are addicted to sin. They love to sit around and plan to do wicked things.

How to deal with wicked imaginations- We deal with imagining wicked things by following Romans 12:2 renewing our mind. We begin to set our mind on things of God and not on things of this world. We take time to think on God's Word, and we pray to God for Him to give us His mind.

5. **Feet that be swift in running to mischief-** This person is quick to rush into doing mischief. They are so eager to commit a sin that they don't walk to the sin they run to it.

How to deal with swift feet- Deal with swift feet by asking God to order your steps Psalm 119:133. We can also get in God's word because His word is a lamp unto our feet and a light to our path. Allow the Holy Spirit to lead us Galatians 5:16 walk in the Spirit, and ye shall not fulfil the lust of the flesh.

6. **False witness that speaketh lies-** We have discussed the lying tongue and the false witness is a liar, but their lie can affect someone's reputation. This type of lying tongue could send an innocent person to jail. This type of lying tongue could cause

someone's life to be taken. In 1 Kings 21 the evil queen Jezebel sent false witness to give a false report about Naboth because her husband King Ahab wanted Naboth's vineyard, but he wasn't willing to give it up. These false witnesses caused Naboth his life.

How to deal with false witness- Learn who you are in Christ and develop your gifts and talents which will leave you no time to spread lies. Also, practice Ephesians 4:29, *"Let no corrupt communication proceed out of your mouth, but that which is good to the use of edifying, that it may minister grace unto the hearers."*

7. **Soweth discord among the brethren-** Discord means a lack of harmony among people. A sower of discord is a person who disrupt harmony among believers. The types of seed they sow in the hearts of others are seeds of hate, distrust, and bitterness. When we sow discord, we are practicing other sins like backbiting and gossiping. Remember Psalm 133:1 says, *"Behold, how good and how pleasant it is for brethren to dwell together in unity!"*

How to deal with a sower of discord- We must practice Ephesians 4:31-32, *"Let all bitterness, and wrath, and anger, and clamor, and evil speaking, be put away from you, with all malice: And be ye kind one to another, tenderhearted, forgiving one another, even as God for Christ's sake hath forgiven you. We have to put away all that anger and gossip, and grudge holding and forgive others just like Christ forgave us."*

In Conclusion, God is a God of love, but there are things that he hates. As believers we should strive not to hurt God. The Bible tells us in Ephesians 4:30, *"Grieve not the Holy Spirit of God, whereby ye are sealed unto the day of redemption."* As a believer, our aim should be to make God happy and to please God.

His word tells us in Revelation 4:11 that, *"We were created for His pleasure. Let us strive to stay away from those things that God hate."*

#THERE ARE THINGS THAT GOD HATES

Appreciating the Blood of Jesus

Ephesians 1:7- In whom we have redemption through his blood, the forgiveness of sins, according to the riches of his grace;

In our world today, the blood of Jesus is not talked about much. Although, His blood is what our entire salvation is based on. In many churches, the blood has been replaced with financial blessing. We have gotten in the habit of having our hand out in the face of God instead of bowing our knees in His presence, thanking him for shedding His blood. Did you know that people participate in Communion Services and give very little attention to what they are doing and why they are doing it?

We, as believers, have lost respect for the blood of Jesus. We do not reflect on what Jesus had to endure for his blood to be shed. We will not appreciate the blood until we begin to reflect on what Jesus Christ endured. We must reflect on Isaiah 53, how Christ's beatings, stripes, chastisement, affliction, and oppression brought us freedom from sin, peace, and healing. We must reflect on his attitude in the midst of all that persecution. He didn't open His mouth. He humbled himself to become sin for us although he knew no sin; so, we can be made right. The Bible tells us in Isaiah 53:10 that it pleased God to bruise Jesus. Jesus knew the cup was going to be heavy because in Matthew 26:39 Jesus asked God if it was possible to let the cup pass from him. Matthew 27 confirmed what Isaiah said would happen to

Jesus. Jesus was stripped and put on a scarlet robe. They placed a crown of thorns on his head. They bowed down mocking him, saying, Hail, King of the Jews! The spit on him. They took a reed and smote him on the head. They gave him vinegar to drink. They then crucified Him. They cast lots for his clothes. Over his head they placed a sign that said THE KING OF THE JEWS. They passed by Jesus on the cross blurting out words like, "save thyself." *"If thou be the Son of God, come down from the cross." "He saved others Himself He cannot save."* Jesus endured all that for us. Romans 5:6 says, *"For when we were yet without strength, in due time Christ died for the ungodly."* He did this for people who were against him. He did it according to 2 Corinthians 5:21 that we might be made the righteousness of God. He did it so mankind could fellowship with God Almighty again. God can communicate to us because of His Son's blood. Because Jesus endured all that, we have many benefits as believers.

BENEFIT 1- Jesus' blood restored our relationship back with God. When man sinned in the garden, our relationship with God was broken; but when Jesus died on that cross and rose from the dead our relationship was restored. Ephesians 2:13 says, *"Now in Christ Jesus ye who sometimes were far off are made nigh by the blood of Jesus Christ."* Romans 5:10 says, *"When we were enemies, we were reconciled to God by the death of his Son, much more being reconciled we shall be save by his life."*

BENEFIT 2- Jesus' blood sanctifies us. That means Jesus' blood set us apart. Hebrews 13:12, let us know Jesus sanctified us with His blood.

BENEFIT 3- Christ's blood provided us with access into God's presence. We no longer have to use a priest to communicate to God for us. The blood of Jesus according to Hebrews 10:19 have given us the boldness to enter in to the holiest. Hebrews 4:6 encourages us to come boldly unto the throne of grace, that we may obtain mercy, and find grace to help in the time of need.

BENEFIT 4- Jesus' blood brings peace. Isaiah 53:5 says, *"The chastisement of our peace was upon Him."* In Luke 2:14, *"The angels declared at His birth he will bring peace to all men."* Colossians 1:20 says, *"Having made peace through the blood of his cross, by him to reconcile all things unto himself."*

BENEFIT 5- *We receive victory through Jesus' blood*. Jesus' blood has given us the victory over any sin, habit, or stronghold that come into our life. 1 Corinthians 15:57 says, *"But thanks be to God, which giveth us the victory through our Lord Jesus Christ."*

In conclusion, Jesus blood is so important for our salvation. If Jesus would not have shed His blood, there would be no remission for sin (Hebrews 9:22). We must learn to appreciate the blood of Christ. We must intentionally think on all that Christ endured for us and all the benefits he gave us because of His shed blood.

#THANK YOU FOR THE BLOOD

Day 17

Watch Out for Idolatry

Exodus 20:5- Thou shalt not bow down thyself to them, nor serve them: for I the Lord thy God am a jealous God.

As a believer, we should make sure idolatry is not creeping up in our lives. Idolatry is worship of idols. Many times, when we think of idols, we think about statues or people worshipping the sun, animals, trees, etc. We hardly look at idolatry as being anything that comes between us and God. At some point in our lives we, all have been guilty of idolatry. There are times we have put other things before God.

We may have put our job, families, hobbies, television, fitness friendships, etc. before God. Did you know that God hates idolatry? God doesn't like us to put anything before him.

Deuteronomy 6:15, let us know that God is a jealous God. God wants our undivided attention but most times we are too busy to give him any attention.

What if God based his action toward me on how I treat him? I wonder why it is so hard to give the Savior of our life, our Shepherd, our provider, God almighty time in our day. We give television time, friend's time, work time, social media time, and etc. It is strange how we make time for everything and everybody, but when it comes to God, we squeeze him in. It is what it is when it comes to God.

Although, He is the giver of life, we assume He should understand that our lives are full. Right?

How can I keep idolatry out of my life?

The only way to keep idolatry out of our lives is to follow Matthew 22:37. Jesus said unto him, *"Thou shalt love the Lord thy god with all thy heart, and with all thy soul, and with all thy mind."* This verse is telling us to love God with all that we are. John 14:15, tells us how we show God we love him. We show God we love him by keeping His commandments. The only way we can keep God's commandments is by learning them. The only way we are going to learn them is by reading the Bible which is the Word of God.

I. Love God with all thy heart

Our heart is our emotion. It is what drives us to do what we do. Jeremiah 17:9 tell us, *"The heart is deceitful above all things, and desperately wicked: who can know it?"* In school we learn various ways to keep our physical heart healthy. We learn ways to keep our heart healthy like exercising, eating right, not smoking, getting rest, etc. Just like we learn ways to keep our physical heart healthy, we must learn ways to keep our spiritually heart healthy:

1. **Make our spiritual life a smoke free environment-** We must separate ourselves from things that will stray us from God. 2 Corinthians 6:17 says, *"Wherefore come out from among them, and be ye separate, saith the Lord, and touch not the unclean things. We must get rid of those things that are slowing us down. To lay aside those things that are hindering our progress for God."*

Today, let us ask ourselves the question: What smoke is clouding our life today? Is it pride, lying, backbiting, complaining, jealousy, etc.?

2. **Eliminate Stress-** How do we eliminate stress from our spiritual lives? We eliminate stress by practicing 1 Peter 5:7 which says, *"Casting all your care upon him; for he careth for you."* and following Matthew 11:28 which says, *"Come unto me, all ye that labour and are heavy laden, and I will give you rest."* We eliminate stress by giving our problems over to Jesus.

3. **Exercise daily-** We exercise daily by developing a quiet time. A quiet time, is a time of no interruptions, a time for just you and God. You talk to God in prayer, and allow him to talk back to you with His word. This should be a daily part of our lives, just like exercising. Physical exercise improves our physical heart health, and spiritual exercise improves our spiritual heart health. Joshua 1:8 let us know if we keep God's word we will be prosperous and have good success. We will have a healthy heart.

II. Love God with all thy soul

Our soul is who we really are. We must love God with our life. God should be the center of our life. We can love God with our life by seeking out the plan He has for our lives. We must get into a position when our plans become obsolete. We must stop creating a plan and create time to spend with the creator who already has a plan for our lives. Jeremiah 29:11 says, *"For I know the plans I have for you declares the Lord, plans to prosper you and not to harm you, plans to give you a hope and a future."* The great thing about loving God with all our soul is that He gives us the plan and He goes with us as we follow our individual designed plan.

III. Love God with all your mind

Don't sit around wasting your mind. We can waste our mind by worrying, being fearful, being jealousy, or being malicious. As I recall teaching school, I would tell my boys and girls to stay on task, get focused, and stop wasting time. As believers, we have to keep our mind stayed and focused on God's word. We have to stop wasting time in our mind. Joyce Meyers once said, "We must begin to think about what we are thinking about."

Remember, God told us to love Him with all our mind, so if I have time to worry that means I am not loving God with all. God wants our mind because our mind drives our action. If my mind is consumed with pleasing God, my actions will produce the character of God. We are instructed in the word of God to renew our mind and to adapt the mind of Christ. The only way we can accomplish this task is by reading God's word. We shouldn't just read God's word, but we must meditate on it and begin applying it to our lives.

In conclusion, as believers we must make sure we are not practicing idolatry. Idolatry is a sin that can be easily ignored because many times we equate idolatry to bowing down to a statue. We don't equate it to bowing down to our money, our jobs, our family, our friends, or our hobbies. The only way we can ensure idolatry is not showing its ugly head in our lives is by loving God with all our heart, soul, and mind.

I CHOOSE TO WORSHIP GOD AND HIM ONLY

Day 18

Dealing with the Seasons of our Life

Ecclesiastes 3:3- To everything there is a season, and a time to every purpose under the heaven

Before you begin this devotional take time to think about the following questions: What is your favorite season of the year and why? Which season is your least favorite and why? Just like we have four seasons a year, believers have seasons throughout their Christian walk.

Spring

I love spring. It seems like everything is new. Everything is growing and all the flowers and trees look beautiful. All believers love spring in their Christian walk. Spring is usually the experience in a believer's life when they first become born again. We are so happy and excited about what God is doing in our life. We have a fresh start and we love it. During this period, we develop an appetite to want more of God's glory and more of him. Spring is also the experience in a believer's life when they are stepping out on a new endeavor. We like the way it feels having that fresh faith in God. It seems as though we are blossoming. It's like our dreams are coming true. During the spring remain grateful.

Summer

Summer is the season when life seems relaxed. We're at a point in which we feel stable. It is a time of vacationing. During the Summer, on the Christian walk, believers sometimes move God to the back burner. They are so busy relaxing in the blessings of God that they forget all about the creator. During the Summer, we should rest in the Lord but we also should spend time planning for the fall and the winter. We should use this time to store up God's word in our heart. We should use this time to memorize verses, to study God's word, to listen to God's word being preached.

Let us not use that time to behave like the grasshopper behaved in the fable of the grasshopper and the ant. In that story, the grasshopper was enjoying Summer so much. He was sipping on his lemonade, playing his banjo and laughing at the ant storing up and preparing for the winter. When winter came, the hard-working ant was relaxing while the grasshopper was trying to find food. Let us not be that believer that is lost looking for direction when winter comes in our life, but let us store up during the Summer.

Remember, Proverbs 6:6 tells us to, *"Go to the ant, thou sluggard; consider her ways, and be wise."*

Fall

Fall is the season of change. This is not one of the believers' favorite season. This season usually brings forth life changes. We may lose our job, a child, a marriage, home, or a friendship. It might be a time when God is prompting you to do something that takes you out of your comfort zone. Everyone hates change because change disrupt our comfort, our familiarity, what we are used to. Doubt usually creeps in during this season. This is a season in which the word of God we stored up on in Summer becomes useful. This is one of those seasons when we have to reflect back on all the new things God was doing in our life during the Spring. This is a time that we should do like James 4:8 says, *"And draw near to God so that he can draw nearer to us."* Do not lose your composure in the fall. Trust God at His word.

Winter

Winter is hard times. Winter is not the time we see all the beautiful flowers and trees. We do not see the beautiful birds flying around and singing. We don't see children chasing after butterflies and fireflies. It is the time in which we see barren trees and grassless grounds. You feel cold temperatures. Winter is a time in which we sometimes feel lonely. During the winter season, we must remember that God is a very present help. We must remember that he will not leave us or forsake us. Winter is the season we spend the Spring and Summer preparing for because sometimes in the Winter of our spiritual life we have to pull out what we have stored up. During Winter, we may become so overwhelmed that our mind is consumed with our problems that we don't know what words to even pray. But if we have stored up God's word, it will come back to our remembrance. We should not go through Summer and Spring forgetting Winter will come.

In conclusion, in life we are going to have some ups and down. We will have some good days and bad days. We will experience times when everything is going great, and those times in which it seems like all is falling apart. I do not know which season of life you are experiencing at this time, but I can encourage you with God's word that no matter what season you are in God will never leave you or forsake you.

God never told us that we will not face trials, but he did promise to always be there. We must remember that our Lord Jesus Christ went through seasons on this earth. His Spring season was his birth. He was born into the world to bring us peace. The shepherds came to worship him. The wise men brought him gifts. At the age of 12, he was speaking things that shocked the Pharisees. He experienced Summer when he began his ministry. He was healing the sick, raising the dead, feeding the hungry, and casting out devils. His season of Fall came in the night leading up to his death. He asked the disciples to pray but they were falling asleep. He asked his Father to let the cup pass from him. He was betrayed by Judas and denied by Peter. He experienced Winter when he was on the cross and his Father had to turn his back on him because he was carrying the sins of the world.

Remember, enjoy your seasons of Spring and Summer, but use those seasons to store up God's word, to sow into other people lives, and to intercede for someone who may be facing a fall or winter.

SEASONS CHANGE

Day 19

I Do Not Fear

Psalm 27:1- The LORD is my light my salvation; whom shall I fear? The Lord is the strength of my life; of whom shall I be afraid?

What are some things people fear? Fear means to be afraid of someone or something that is likely to be dangerous, painful, or threatening. Psalm 27 lets us know that *God is our light.* We know that we use a light for direction. We use a light to be able to see in a dark place. God is our guide. He brightens up our way. In John 8:12, Jesus said, *"I am the light of the word."* As long as God is our light we don't have to fear because he is ordering our steps in the right direction. The Bible lets us know that the word of God is a light. Psalm 119:105, let us know *"God's word is a lamp unto my feet, and a light unto my path."* We allow God to be the light in our life when we begin to acknowledge him in all our ways. When we do that, he directs our life. He directs us to the plan He already prepared for our life. Walking in darkness stops God from being our light because. darkness and light cannot fellowship. 1 John 1:7 says, *"If we walk in the light as He is in the light, we have fellowship one with another."* We can only fellowship with God when we are allowing Him to be the light of our life.

Psalm 27 also lets us know that *God is our salvation.* Salvation is deliverance from sin and consequences. Salvation is also deliverance from harm, ruin, or loss. This lets me know that God protects. This should keep us from worrying about our past, present and future because God will protect us. God comes to our dark situations and rescues us out of them. The greatest situation God ever rescued mankind from, was sin.

God became flesh and dwelt among us to save us from sin. He sent Jesus to save us from His wrath. Acts 4:12 tells us, *"Neither is there salvation in any other: for there is none other name under heaven given among men, whereby we must be saved."* God is our strength. Strength means being strong or having power. The opposite of strength is weakness.

In 2 Corinthians 12:9 Paul says, *"...when I am weak he makes me strong".* Have you ever prayed the prayer Lord give me strength? God is saying, *I am your strength.* He is saying rest in me and let me be your strength. In society, a strong person is viewed as a person who can carries their own load, an independent person. In God's eyes, a strong person is one who is totally dependent on God and only relies on Him. Whenever you find yourself doubting, grumbling or complaining, you are not allowing God to be your strength. When it seems as though you are getting weak, remember Psalm 28:7 which says, *"The Lord is my strength and my shield."* Psalm 46:1 reads, *"God is our refuge and strength, a very present help in trouble."* At times when you feel you are about to faint, take joy in the Lord. The joy of the Lord is our strength and remember you can do all things through Christ which strengthened you.

In conclusion, we do not have to fear things as long as we keep God as our light, salvation, and strength.

That means God is our direction, protection, and power.

I DO NOT FEAR

Day 20

Tug of War: The Fight of the Two Natures

Romans 5:19- For as by one man's disobedience many were made sinners, so by the obedience of one shall many be made righteous.

Once we allow Christ to come into our lives, we inherit a new nature which causes us to have two natures. We have the old nature that we are born with because of the sin of Adam. When we are born again, we receive the new nature because of the obedience of Christ. The old nature and the new nature is in constant battle because they both want to be the controlling force of your life. Galatians 5:17 says, *"The flesh lusteth against the Spirit, and the Spirit against the flesh: and these are contrary the one to the other: so you cannot do the things that ye would."*

Whenever you see flesh in the Bible remember that it is referring to the old nature. According to Roman 8:7, the old nature is an enemy to God, so whenever we are allowing the flesh to take over we can't please God. As believers, we must strive to do those things that will keep the new nature in control. The only way we can keep the new nature in control is to obey Galatians 5:16 and *walk in the Spirit*. If we do not walk in the Spirit, we will become a slave to the old nature.

Walking in the Spirit is when we allow the Holy Spirit to take control of our life. Our thoughts, motives and desires no longer matter. Christ wants to be Lord over all. He wants to be Lord over our attitudes, finances, relationships, health, and decisions.

Remember, once we become a Christian, we no longer belong to ourselves. Galatians 6:19 says we are not our own. The Spirit can only control our lives when we choose to let Him. The Spirit does not force His way into our lives. He only controls a totally surrendered life.

Surrender means we yield up all our control to Christ. That means all of our decisions are based on God's word. A person who has totally surrendered to Christ has their heart and mind set on things above. They have put to death all those earthly desires. What are the earthly desires?

The earthly desires are found in Galatians 5:19-21, sexual immorality, impure thoughts, eagerness for lustful pleasure, idolatry, participation in demonic activities, hostility, quarreling, jealousy, outburst of anger, selfish ambition and division. The feeling that everyone is wrong except those in your own little group, envy, drunkenness, wild parties, and other kinds of sin. These desires should be replaced with the fruit of the Spirit found in Galatians 5:22-23. The fruit of the spirit is love, joy, peace, longsuffering, gentleness, goodness, faith, meekness, and temperance.

The only way the fruit which is Christ can replace those earthly desires is by walking in the Spirit. We will confidently let the new nature be in control if we constantly remember that we already have the victory. 1 Corinthians 15:57, lets us know that we have victory through Jesus Christ. Romans 8:37 lets us know we are more than conquerors.

We must also remember God will keep us if we allow Him to do so. If we keep in mind that we already have the victory, it will become easy for us to take off the old man and put on the new one. The more we yield to Christ, the brighter His personality will shine in our lives. We must begin to give Christ the right to guide our lives. We must begin to pray prayers like:

Psalm 19:12- *Cleanse me from secret faults*

Psalm 119:33- *Teach me, O Lord, the way of thy statues*

Psalm 119:133- *Order my steps in your word*

Psalm 141:3- *Set a watch, O LORD, before my mouth; keep the door of my lips.*

In conclusion, we have two natures. These two natures are in constant war with each other. We must make a choice as believers to let Christ be the head controller of our life. We do this by surrendering to his will. We will find His will in the word of God. When we allow Christ to be the controller, our lives change. Our personality, attitudes, thoughts, desires, and habits change. We become that new creation mentioned in 2 Corinthians 5:17.

We must allow Christ to coach our life. We learn His plan by reading the Word, and if we begin to trust Him with our all, we will see our life transform. The difference will be noticed by you and others around you.

THERE'S A WAR GOING ON

Day 21

A very Present Help in Trouble

Psalm 46:1- God is our refuge and strength, a very present help in trouble.

⌁

Have you ever asked the question why God or when God? Have you ever been in a situation and you were just ready for this stage or season in life to be over. Well, today let me encourage you with God being a very present help in trouble. God never stated we wouldn't have trouble.

Actually, in John 16:33, He lets us know in the world we will have tribulations (problems, and difficult circumstances), but be of good cheer because Christ have overcome the world. He even reminds us that we are overcomers in 1 John 4 because we have the greater, which is Christ, in us. Psalm 46:1 says, *"God is our refuge and strength, a very present help in trouble."*

A refuge is a hiding place. It feels good knowing that God will hide us. The verse also lets us know that God is our strength. He is our power and He makes us strong. God gives us the power to face our problems and circumstances. The next thing the verse lets us know is that He is a present help. Present means right there. God is Omnipresent. He is everywhere. Psalm 139: 7-10 talks about God Omnipresence.

Those verses let us know we cannot escape God's presence. The Psalmist says if he ascends up into the heaven, God is there. If he makes his bed in hell, God is there. He finally says if he dwells by the farthest ocean, God is there.

Proverbs 15:3 further describes God's Omnipresence by letting us know that the Lord's eyes are in every place, beholding the evil and the good. Finally, the verse lets us know that He is that present help in trouble. Some of life's troubles are financial problems, health issues, relationship problems, problems on our job, etc.

When trouble comes in our lives, we must rest on God's word.

Rely on scriptures like Psalm 30:5, *"Weeping may endure for a night, but joy cometh in the morning."*

Rest in Romans 8:28, *"And we know that all things work together for good to them that love God, to them who are called according to his purpose."*

Rely on Matthew 19:26, *"With God all things are possible."*

Our refuge asks us to call on him when we are in trouble and he said he will answer. Jeremiah 33:3 says, *"Call unto me, and I will answer thee, and shew thee great and mighty things, which thou knowest not."*

Psalm 50:15 says, *"Call upon me in the day of trouble: I will deliver thee, and thou shalt glorify me."* And finally John 6:37, Jesus tell us to come to Him and He, in no wise will cast us out.

When we allow God to be our refuge, we have to totally depend on Him and not rely on ourselves. Did you know God is more glorified in our weakness because His strength is on display because He makes us strong? We truly will receive liberty from worrying when we become totally dependent on God.

One of my favorite Bible stories that displays God being a refuge and strength... a very present help in trouble is found in 2 Chronicles 20. In this story, we are introduced to a king by the name of Jehoshaphat. In this story three armies were coming against Judah. King Jehoshaphat became fearful. He knew that they were in trouble. He knew the only thing he could do was seek God, and he did. He proclaimed a fast throughout all of Judah. They called on God for help.

Although, our God knows all and is everywhere, he still wants us to come to Him and tell Him our problems. As they fasted and prayed, the Spirit of the Lord came upon Jahaziel. Jahaziel told the people that God said be not afraid or dismayed. He said, the Lord said they will not have to fight the battle because the battle is the Lord's. He told them to set themselves, stand still and see the salvation of the Lord. God delivered them through praise and worship. God was a refuge and a very present help in the time of Judah's troubles.

What battles in your life have you afraid or dismayed? Today, I encourage you to give that battle to God. Remember, God has already won the victory for us.

In conclusion, God is a very present help in trouble. When it seems like the walls are closing in on us and everything around us is falling apart, hang on to the hope that God is our right now help in trouble.

Remember, God is never caught by surprise even in those situations that looks completely hopeless. God's word lets us know he will never leave us nor forsake us. Just like He helped King Jehoshaphat and Judah he will help us, but we have to call on him.

A Very Present Help in Trouble

Day 22

What Is Your Impossible?

Luke 1:37- For with God nothing shall be impossible.

I mpossible means something that is very difficult to deal with. We all have come across situations that seem impossible to us, but today I want you to know there is no situation impossible for God. We have several scriptures in the Bible that let us know there is nothing impossible for God.

In Genesis 18:14, God asked the question, *"Is there anything too hard for the Lord?"*

In Jeremiah 32:17, God said, *"There is nothing too hard for the Lord."* Luke 1:37 says, *"For with God nothing shall be impossible."* And finally Matthew 19:26 says *"With men this is impossible, but with God all things are possible."*

What is your impossible? What is that thing that always tries to invade your mind? What is that thing that is trying to keep you depressed? In the Bible there are various people who faced impossible situations. The woman with the issue of blood in Mark 5 was faced with an impossible situation. This woman had a blood issue for 12 years. She had gotten to the point where she'd spent all she had going to doctors, but instead of her condition getting better her condition got worse. This woman heard that Jesus was in her midst, so she went and touch his garment because she had said, if I may touch but his clothes, I shall be whole. When she touched Jesus, she was made whole. This lady had an impossible situation and she had it 12 years. Her impossible situation was just right for God because when she touched Jesus' garment, she was made whole.

You might be saying within yourself that she was right there in the presence of Jesus, so her condition dried up. You might be wondering how you can touch Jesus' garment today. Well, today we can touch his garment by trusting His word.

Remember, Jesus was the Word made flesh. His word tells us in 1 Peter 5:7, to cast all our cares upon him for he careth for you. Philippians 4:19, tells us that God will supply all our needs. No matter what our impossible situation is, we must learn to trust God with it and acknowledge Him in all our ways.

In conclusion, we will have situations that come up in our life. Yes, sometimes these situations will seem impossible. These situations will sometimes make us question God asking him why me? Do you see me, God? When will this all end?

In these times, God wants us to remember him as the possible God. He wants us to have faith in Him like the woman with the issue of blood who believed that if she could just touch His garment she would be made whole. He wants us to have faith in him and not become fearful during those times. He wants us to remember verses like 2 Timothy 1:7 that God did not give us the Spirit of fear; but of power, and of love, and of sound mind.

ALL THINGS ARE POSSIBLE

Day 23

Fearing God

~~~~~~~~

Ecclesiastes 12:13–Let us hear the conclusion of the whole matter: Fear God, and keep his commandments: for this is the whole duty of man.

Believers are not afraid of God. God does not want us to be scared of him. So, what does the Bible mean when it tells us to fear God? Fearing God is to show respect and reverence to God. We fear God by obeying and worshipping Him. We fear God by honoring him in all we do. The Bible lets us know that fearing God brings wisdom.

Psalm 111:10 says, *"The fear of the LORD is the beginning of wisdom."*

Proverbs 1:7 tells us, *"The fear of the Lord is the beginning of knowledge."*

Proverbs 9:10, *"Tells us the fear of the Lord is the foundation of wisdom."*

God's word commands us to fear him. Deuteronomy 10:12 says, *"What doth the Lord require of thee, but to fear the Lord thy God, to walk in all his ways, and to love him, and to serve the Lord thy God with all thy heart and with all thy soul."* It is repeated again, in Deuteronomy 10:20, *"Thou shalt fear the Lord thy God; him shalt thou serve, and to him shalt thou cleave, and swear by name."*

How do I begin to fear God?

Recognize God as the creator. We must remember that God created everything. Genesis 1:1 let us know that God created heaven and earth in the beginning. Colossians 1:16 says, *"For by him were all things created, that are in heaven, and that are in earth, visible and invisible, whether they be thrones, or dominions, or principalities, or powers: all things were created by him, and for him."* And John 1:3 says, *"Through him all things were made; without him nothing was made that has been made."*

Have respect for His word. Respecting God's word is a sign that we fear God. We must take time to read his word. We must begin to mediate on His word day and night, and begin to apply his word to our life. Applying his word to our life will protect us. It will keep us from sinning against God. As we read God's word we learn more about His character. We learn who He is which will cause us to fear him.

We will learn that He is Holy, and He cannot dwell in ungodliness. We will learn that He is all knowing and that nothing shocks or surprises Him, and that He is incapable of learning. He can't learn anything. He knows all.

In the book of Deuteronomy, the kings were required to write out a copy of God's law and spend time each day reading it so that they would learn to fear the Lord. Check out Deuteronomy 17:18-19, *"And it shall be, when he sitteth upon the throne of his kingdom, that he shall write him a copy of this law in a book out of that which is before the priests the Levites: And it shall be with him, and he shall read therein all the days of his life: that he may learn to fear the Lord his God, to keep all the words of this law and these statutes, to do them:*

Benefits of fearing God

He will give you your heart's desire- Psalm 145:19, "He will fulfill the desire of them that fear him; he will also hear their cry and will save them."

You are prosperous- Psalm 25:12-13, *"What man is he that feareth the Lord? Him shall he teach in the way that he shall choose. His souls shall dwell at ease; and his seed shall inherit the earth."*

Experience God's Protection- Psalm 31:19-20, *"Oh how great is thy goodness, which thou hast laid up for them that fear thee; which thou hast wrought for them that trust in thee before the sons of men! Thou shalt hide them in the secret of thy presence from the pride of man: thou shalt keep them secretly in a pavilion from the strife of tongues."*

Blessed with wisdom- Proverbs 9:10- *"The fear of the Lord is the beginning of wisdom."*

Called Blessed- Psalm 112:1- *"Praise ye the Lord, Blessed is the man that feareth the Lord, that delight greatly in his commandments."*

Receive riches and Honor- Proverbs 22:4- *"By humility and the fear of the Lord are riches, honour, and life."*

Angels surround you- Psalm 34:7- *"The angel of the Lord encampeth round about them that fear him, and delivereth him."*

Salvation- Psalm 85:9- "Surely his salvation is nigh them that fear him; that glory may dwell in our land."

Long life- Proverbs 10:27- "The fear of the Lord prolongeth days."

In conclusion, fearing God is respecting and honoring him. We respect God by obeying his Word and we learn to obey by reading his Word. We must remember God commanded us to fear him. Ecclesiastes 12:13, *"Let us hear the conclusion of the whole matter: Fear God, and keep his commandments: for this is the whole duty of man."*

I FEAR GOD

Day 24

Seek God First

Matthew 6:33- But seek ye first the kingdom of God and his righteousness and all these things shall be added unto you.

As believers, we must learn to seek God first. We spend so much time trying to get things like food, clothes, and shelter, but the word of God says if we seek him first everything else is an add on.

In Matthew 6:25, Jesus was teaching and in this lesson, He said take no thoughts for your life, what ye shall eat, or what ye shall drink. He uses the birds as an example. He talks about how they are not going around worrying and how God takes care of the birds and we are much greater than the birds.

In verse 33, He tells us to seek the kingdom of God and His righteousness. As believers, we must stop seeking financial blessings, health blessings, cars, houses, and better jobs, but we must begin to seek God's Kingdom and his righteousness. The kingdom of God is bigger than us. It is not just about us.

We have confused seeking God's kingdom with seeking things. If most of your prayers are for you and for natural things, you are not seeking God's kingdom. When we seek out God's kingdom, attention leaves the circle of me, myself, and I. When you seek the kingdom of God you are not longing for natural blessings. Natural blessings are things like financial breakthroughs, healing for your body or someone else body, praying for success, praying about stress on the job, and etc. All these requests are good, but those are all add-ons.

When we seek God, our goal is to advance God's ministry. Our prayers go from bless me indeed to Lord save and deliver lost souls. You begin to seek out ways to minister to people. You pray for God to give you a greater understanding of his Word, so that you can encourage people.

When we are seeking God, we are creating more time in our schedule to spend with God instead of making up excuses why we can't spend any time with him. As believers, we must spend less time crying and asking God for those things that will be added on to us. Satan loves that most believers have gotten so hooked on prosperity. We have gotten so used to pulling down blessing, marching around houses and cars, and trying to speak things into existence that we forgot all about the work of the ministry.

We forgot all about the great commission of going into all the world and preaching the gospel and then teaching the ones that come to Christ how to observe all things. It is such a shame that believers will go on a seven day fast for a new car but will not pray seven days for souls to be saved or for the anointing Peter had that by being in his shadow healing took place. How often do we pray for God to take fear from us so we can preach his word with boldness? How often do we pray for God to make people attentive to his Word? How often do we pray for God to give us His heart and His mind? How many times have we asked God to make whatever hurt him hurt us? Let us stop doing so many things to obtain natural blessings, but let us strive to those things that draws us to seeking God. Let us begin to:

Commit to Him- Psalm 37:5 says, *"Commit thy way unto the Lord; trust also in him; and he shall bring it to pass."*

Delight in him- Psalm 37:4- *"Delight thyself also in the Lord: and he shall give thee the desires of thine heart."*

Abide in him- John 15:7- *"If ye abide in me, and my words abide in you, ye shall ask what ye will, and it shall be done unto you."*

Meditate on His law- Psalm 1:2- *"But his delight is in the law of the Lord; and in his law doth he meditates day and night."*

Walk uprightly- Psalm 84:11- *"For the Lord God is a sun and shield: The Lord will give grace and glory: No good thing will he withhold from them that walk uprightly."*

Be unified- Matthew 18:19- *"Again I say unto you, That if two of you shall agree on earth as touching anything that they shall ask, it shall be done for them of my Father which is in heaven…"*

Tell others about Jesus- Mark 16:16, *"Go ye into all the world, and preach the gospel."*

In conclusion, our blessings are not going to come from us turning around, marching around, and trying to pull down a blessing from the heavens. Our blessing will come when we begin to seek God's kingdom and his righteousness. Seeking God is pursuing after him by doing the ministry.

I WILL SEEK GOD FIRST

Day 25

Preparing for Revival

Psalm 85:6- Wilt thou not revive us again: that thy people may rejoice in thee?

Prepare means to make someone or something ready. In life, we prepare for many things. We prepare for our careers. We prepare for a wedding. We prepare for a new baby. We prepare for vacation, for family reunions, and for weddings.

It is strange how much time we spend preparing for all these earthly things that will pass away and we spend very little time preparing for what will be eternal our soul. As believers, we must not become so attached to this world, because everything in this world is temporal. We must remember that only our relationship with God and our service to him will last forever.

Revive means to refresh to give new strength and new energy. Have you ever said the phrase, "We are having revival"? To most of us, this is just a 3 day or a week-long meeting that takes place at 7:00 pm. Many times, we go to revival expecting to receive something from God. We want God to do something for us without preparing to receive from Him.

How do I prepare for revival?

2   Chronicles 7:14 tells us how to prepare for revival. It says, *"If my people, which are called by my name, shall humble themselves, and pray, and seek my face, and turn from their wicked ways; then will I hear from heaven and will forgive their sin, and will heal their land."* This verse tells believers to do four things:

Humble themselves- We must humble ourselves which means to show low estimate of one's own importance. We must break away from our pride and humble ourselves enough to tell God we are sorry for our sin. We need to ask God to forgive us for been lazy in reading His word, praying, and sharing the gospel with others. We need to ask God to forgive us for not striving to keep unity in the body of Christ. Forgive us for neglecting the gift or gifts He has given us for the work of the ministry and for the edifying of the body of Christ. We must humbly ask God for forgiveness in order to experience revival.

Pray- Prayer is communicating with God. As believers, we must begin to pray. It is easy to talk about and to preach about prayer, but it takes commitment and perseverance to actually pray. We must become intentional about praying. We must start planning what we are going to pray about to God. We should have a purpose in praying to God. Do you ever plan what you going to pray to God? Jeremiah 33:3 tells us to, *"Call on me and I will answer and show thee great and mighty things."*

Do you find yourself complaining more than calling on God? In order for us to experience, revival we must pray a prayer of brokenness like Nehemiah prayed in Nehemiah 1. When we pray with a sincere broken heart to God, the Bible tells us in Psalm 51:17 that God will not despise or reject a broken heart.

SEEK GOD'S FACE- We must strive to be in God's presence. God has invited us to seek His face. The Bible tells us in Matthew 6:33, *"But seek ye first the kingdom of God, and his righteousness; and all these things shall be added unto you."* Seeking God is getting in His thoughts, and discovering how He feels about different things. God wants us to feel how He feels about sin. He wants us to see and feel His love and compassion. He wants us to constantly have His word on our mind.

Colossians 3:1-2 tells us *"If ye then be risen with Christ, seek those things which are above, where Christ sitteth on the right hand of God. Set your affection on things above, not on things on the earth."* When we seek God, our aim is to put a smile on Jesus' face. Do my actions put a smile on Jesus' face? As believers, we must strive to seek God. Jeremiah 29:13 says. *"And ye shall seek me, and find me, when ye shall search for me with all your heart. If we seek God with our whole heart, He will be found."*

TURN FROM OUR WICKED WAYS- To turn means to change. A caterpillar turns into a butterfly. It experiences transformation. As believers, we must turn our attitudes and behavior from sin into God's righteousness. In order for us to experience revival, we must drop off those sins that are separating us from Christ. Hebrews 12:1, tells us to, *"Lay aside every weight, and the sin which doth so easily beset* *us, and let us run with patience the race that is set before us."* We must realize that salvation is free, but to grow in our faith will take hard work. This life requires us to let go of those things that will jeopardize or put at risk our relationship with God. Don't ignore those small things that we call our personalities. We must lay those things away as well. We must lay aside pride, selfishness, complaining, unforgiveness, bitterness, and anger. Those are things we try to make excuses for why it is ok for us to hold on to them.

If we want God to hear from heaven and bring healing to our land, our wicked ways have to be thrown out of our life. When God highlights the sin in our life, we need to drop it. In 2 Kings, chapters 22-23, when King Josiah and God's people heard God's word, they realized they were not following God's word. They turned from their evil ways to God. King Josiah told Hilkiah, the high priest, to go into the temple and bring all the vessels made for Baal and burn them. These people made the choice to turn from their wicked ways and turn back to God. Just like they had to clean the temple of God, we have to do the same.

1 Corinthians 6:19 tells us that our body is the temple of God, and as believers we must do some temple cleansing. Get rid of idols such as greed, hate, lust, lying, gossiping, pride, selfishness, and anything that God calls sin. In order for God to revive us we have to get rid of idols. Is there anything that has all of your time, and is causing you to have no time with God? Are things like television, Facebook, Instagram, friends, work, and sometimes even ministry taking up your time? What has all your attention? If your answer is not God

you must remove that idol from your life in order to experience revival.

In conclusion, it is time for God's people to experience revival not just another service or a good feeling. It is time for us to humble before God. It is time for us to pray, to seek God's face, and turn from our wicked ways. It is time for us to seek God until He comes and rain righteousness in our lives (Hosea 10:12).

God is incapable of lying. He said if we, His people, will humble ourselves, pray, seek His face and turn from His wicked ways that he will hear from heaven, forgive our sin, and heal our land. God is ready to send healing and deliverance, but are we willing to use the prescription He prescribed.

#Revive Me

Day 26

God's Waiting Room

Lamentation 3:25- The LORD is good unto them that wait for him, to the soul that seeketh him.

I recall reading an article by Joyce Meyers. In her article, she asked the readers several questions. Some of the questions were: Have you been praying about a situation in your life and found yourself waiting for a breakthrough? Are you wondering why the answer hasn't come yet? Do you feel that victory is passing by you? To wait means to stay where one is or to delay action until a particular time. In life waiting is something we all have to do.

We have to wait in line at the store. We have to wait to be seen by the doctor. We have to wait to graduate from high school. Mothers have to wait nine months to deliver a baby. Waiting is just part of our life. It is not just part of our natural life, but it is also a part of our spiritual life. Many times, God makes us wait for things, and to be honest, waiting is not one of our greatest past times. We usually do not take great joy in waiting. The Bible tells us in Psalm 27:14 to, "Wait on the Lord: be of good courage, and he shall strengthen thine heart: wait, I say, on the Lord."

How to wait on God

Let us take a few minutes to think about the things we do while waiting in the line at the grocery store, or waiting to see the doctor, or even waiting on the beautician to style our hair. While we are waiting, we may text a friend, scroll down our Facebook page, play a game, complete a cross word puzzle, send out an email, etc. We try to find something to occupy our time as we wait. As we wait on God for our breakthrough, we need to find something to occupy our mind. How you ever been in a car on a long road trip with small children? Every few minutes they are asking the question, "Are we there yet? "Eventually a parent will put a movie on or give the child something to occupy their time. I often wonder how often we sound like those small children asking God the question, "Am I there yet? Lord, is it over? As believers, we should be occupying our minds. You may be wondering, "How I can occupy my time as I wait on God?"

Fill up on his word- The greatest thing we can do while waiting on God is to read his word. His word is filled with promises and stories of people who waited on him. God's word will encourage us as we read it while waiting. God's word will also build our faith because His word is certain. His word will not return to him void, so we can have complete confident in His word. The more time we spend reading his word in the waiting room, the less time we will have to worry or to constantly ask him is the wait over.

Continue to work our gift- As we wait on God, we must remain a good servant for Him. I often think about the people in Jeremiah's days. The people of God were in bondage because of their sins. While in bondage, they waited for God's deliverance. They had to continue to work. As you wait on God, search out ways to minister to other people and ways to show kindness to others. Don't become a selfish waiter, but be a generous waiter. Find ways to bless others during your wait.

Remember, as you bless others you are preparing for your blessing. Luke 6:38, NLT, *"Give, and you will receive."* Your gift will return to you in full- pressed down, shaken together to make room for more, running over, and poured into your lap. The amount you give will determine the amount you get back. After reading that, all I can say is wow!!!! No one can beat God's giving. We must remember whatever we give out that is what going to come back in full. If I give out compassion, love, time, money, and kindness, that's what I will receive. If I give out slothfulness, complaining, selfishness, and neglect, that's what I will receive. As you wait on God, monitor yourself to see what you are giving out.

Continue to call on God- As you wait on God, remain prayerful. Do not let the wait distract you from calling on the one who is right there with you in the wait. Jeremiah 33:3, tell us to call unto the Lord and he will answer us and show us great and mighty things. Many times, we spend more time talking to people about our problem during the wait and no time talking to the problem solver. As we wait on God, spend time talking to him. Talk to him about His word and His promises.

Remember that God has a plan for you- Remember as you wait, God is the one that designed this plan for you. He is not surprised that you are in His waiting room. We must remember that waiting at this time was already in God's plan. Jeremiah 29:11 says, *"For I know the plans I have for you, declares the LORD plans to prosper you and not to harm you, plans to give you a hope and a future."*

In conclusion, we might ask God many questions while waiting in His waiting room. We might ask him: Will this ever end? Do you hear me calling you? Have you forgotten me Lord? God is answering all our questions with these scriptures.

Proverbs 3:5-6- *Trust in the Lord with all thine heart; and lean not unto thine own understanding. In all thy ways acknowledge him, and he shall direct thy paths.*

Romans 8:28- *And we know that all things work together for good to them that love God, to them who are the called according to his purpose.*

Psalm 46:1- *God is our refuge and strength, a very present help in trouble*

Psalm 54:4 (NIV)- *Surely God is my help; the Lord is the one who sustains me*

1 Thessalonians 5:18- *In everything give thanks: for this is the will of God in Christ Jesus concerning you.*

Hebrews 10:23- *Let us hold fast the profession of our faith without wavering; (for he is faithful that promised;)*

Waiting is not always fun. I read this quote one day on Facebook and it said Joseph waited 15 years, Abraham waited 25 years, Moses waited 40 years, and Jesus waited 30 years to start his ministry, and then waited 3 more years to do what he came to earth to do which was die for our sin. We must also remember God waited. In Genesis 3:15, God spoke of Jesus being our blood sacrifice. It was not until the New Testament when Jesus was the last lamb God slain for our sins. We must learn to wait on God patiently. We must remember scriptures like Isaiah 40:31- *"But they that wait upon the Lord shall renew their strength; they shall mount up with wings as eagles; they shall run, and not be weary; and they shall walk, and not faint"* and Psalm 119:114, *"Thou art my hiding place and my shield: I hope in thy word."*

God's Waiting Room

Stay on Task

Colossians 3:2- *Set your affection on things above, not on things on the earth.*

When I taught school, students would often get off task. I would sometimes find students day dreaming, fidgeting, doodling on paper and some were even bold enough to carry on a conversation. They were busy doing things that were not connected to their assignment.

As believers, we must make sure we are staying on task and keeping up with the assignment God has given us. What is your assignment from God? Are you working on your assignment or are you distracted from it? In the book of Jonah, God gave Jonah an assignment. His assignment was to go in warn the people of Nineveh of their wickedness. Jonah, because of his dislike for the people, chose to get off task. He went the opposite direction of where God told him to go. Jonah allowed prejudice and dislike to get him off of task. What is causing you to get off task of your assignment to God? Is it fear? Is it family or friends? Is it your job? Is it money? Is it pride? What has you off task?

As believers, we must strive to stay on task. There are some things all of God's children should be on task doing. All God's children should be:

PRAYING- We should always be on task by talking to God about our situation and the situations of others. 1 Thessalonians 5:17, tells us to *pray without ceasing* and Colossians 4:2 tells us to *continue in prayer.*

You may be wondering what we should be praying. We should be praying God's word right back to Him. We should be praying Colossians 4:3, that God open up doors for us to speak the mystery of Christ. We should be praying Colossians 1:9-10, that we might be filled with the knowledge of his will in all wisdom and spiritual understanding, that we live a life that pleases God, and that we are fruitful in every good works and increasing in God's knowledge.

We should be praying Philippians 1:9-11 that our *love may abound, that we be filled with the fruits of righteousness.* We should be praying Ephesians 1:17-19 that God give us the *spirit of wisdom* and revelation in the knowledge of him, that the eyes of our understanding be enlightened, and pray that we know the hope of our calling. We should be praying Matthew 5:6, that God give us a hunger and thirst after righteousness.

Finally, we should be praying Psalm 119:18 that God will open up our eyes that we behold wondrous things out of his law.

GIVING THANKS- 1 Thessalonians 5:18 says, *"In everything give thanks: for this is the will of God in Christ Jesus concerning you."* In the world today, it is easy to become ungrateful. Being unthankful is one of the attitudes that will be seen during the last days according to 2 Timothy 3. God is encouraging his children to stay on task by giving thanks to Him. There are some things that should stay on our mind to help us keep an attitude of thanksgiving:

REMEMBER GOD'S LOVE- 1 Chronicles 16:34- *O give thanks unto the Lord; for he is good; for his mercy endureth forever.*

REMEMBER GOD'S SPECIAL GIFT- 2 Corinthians 9:15- *Thanks be unto God for his unspeakable gift*

REMEMBER GOD'S VICTORY- 1 Corinthians 15:57- *But thanks be unto God, which giveth us the victory through our Lord Jesu Christ.*

REMEMBER GOD'S MARVELOUS WORK- Psalm 9:1- *I will praise thee, O LORD, with my whole heart, I will shew forth all thy marvelous works.*

We must remember that it is impossible to be grateful and to complain at the same time. Whenever we find ourselves in a state of discontentment we are no longer giving God thanks. We have allowed Psalm 96:4 to slip our mind. The Psalm says the Lord is great, and greatly to be praise.

LIVING A LIFE THAT PLEASES GOD- 1 Thessalonians 4:1 tells us to *live a life that is pleasing to God.* As believers, we must ask ourselves questions. One question we should daily asked is, am I doing anything that doesn't please God? We should make sure we are not grieving the Holy Spirit. The way we grieve God's spirit is by operating in sin. Sin blocks our intimate relationship with God. Psalm 66:18 says if I regard iniquity in my heart the Lord will not hear me. Our daily prayers should be Psalm 139:23-24, *"Search me, O God, and know my heart: try me, and know my thoughts: And see if there be any wicked way in me, and lead me in the way everlasting."* Below are a few questions from Heather Holleman's book, *Seated With Christ*, that we can use as a guide to keep us living a life pleasing to God:

A. Does this activity bring me closer to Jesus or further away?
B. Is this activity forbidden in scripture?
C. Does this activity help others know Jesus?
D. Would I be embarrassed if Jesus arrived and saw me doing this activity?
E. How do I feel about myself and my relationship with God after doing this activity?

In conclusion, we must remain focused. Let us stay on task. Do not allow things to distract you from your purpose in Christ. Keep your eyes fixed on God. This is done by staying in His word. Make it a habit to study God's word. Constantly pray and ask God to teach you His word and to help you to abide in His word. Stay focused! Stay engaged with the things of God. When I taught school, I had to read a book titled, *Teach like a Champion.* This book provided several strategies to keep students engaged during the lesson. One strategy that was given was called SLANT. SLANT means

Sit up
Listen
Ask and answer questions
Nod your head
Track the speaker

I begin to wonder how I can use SLANT to remind me to stay focus on God's word. This is what I came up with:

Set a time to spend with God
Listen to God as he speaks to you
Ask God questions by praying and receive your answer from His word
Navigate through God's word to learn His character
Teach others what you learned about God

#STAY FOCUSED

Day 28

In the Center of His Will

Ecclesiastes 12:13- Let us hear the conclusion of the whole matter: Fear God, and keep his commandments: for this is the whole duty of man.

The center is the focus point. We must remember that God's will is a place of safety. Psalm 91:1 says, "He that dwelleth in the secret place of the most High shall abide under the shadow of the Almighty. We will abide in that safe place if we abide in God's will.

How do we get into God's Will?

Have you ever said the phrase, "I hope I am in God's will?" Here are some ways to know you are in God's will:

ACKNOWLEDGE GOD- Proverbs 3:6 tells us to *acknowledge God in all our ways and he shall direct thy path.* To acknowledge God means to recognize and accept His existence. We acknowledge God by getting His approval on the decisions we are making. The opposite of acknowledging is ignoring. When we do not acknowledge God before we make decisions, we are ignoring God's authority in our life. The benefit of acknowledging God is he give us guidance. God is our best guide for our life because Jeremiah 29:11 let us know he has our life's plan. When we acknowledge God, we are turning every area of our life over to Him. We are relinquishing all of our control. Before you move on, examine your life and see if there are any areas you have not given over to God. What areas of your life have you not acknowledged God?

Biblical Example of Acknowledging God and not Acknowledging God

The character Joshua was known for acknowledging God. In Joshua 3, before the Israelites crossed the Jordan, Joshua acknowledged God, and he was given instruction from God on how to cross. In Joshua 6, Joshua acknowledged God before they conquered Jericho. God gave Joshua direct instructions on how to conquer Jericho. In both of these cases, Joshua acknowledged God and was successful. In Joshua 7, we see where Joshua did not acknowledge God before trying to conquer Ai. The people told Joshua that they would only need 2 or 3 thousand soldiers to destroy Ai, so Joshua sent them out to fight. When they went out to fight, 36 of the men were killed.

The small city of Ai had God's people running. Joshua cried out to God, and asked God why he allowed them to cross the Jordan if he was going to allow the Amorites to kill them. God told Joshua to get up off his knees. God said Israel has sinned and broken my covenant. If Joshua would have acknowledged God before going to Ai, God would have told him about the sin of Achan, but instead of Joshua acknowledging God he became so pumped up in their victory over Jericho that he was ready to defeat the next Army. In Joshua chapter 8, God told Joshua to take all the people of war and go up to Ai, remember the people told him to take 2 or 3 thousand. We must remember to acknowledge God in all our ways, because He will lead us to victory.

GIVE THANKS- 1 Thessalonians 5:18 says, *"In everything give thanks; for this is the will of God in Christ Jesus."* When we give thanks, we are in God's will. The opposite of giving thanks is complaining, grumbling, and worrying. No matter what situation or circumstance comes in our lives, we must learn to give God thanks. Giving thanks to God keeps us humble. It reminds us that we can't do anything on our own. Giving thanks also reminds us of the things we do have. Many times, we overshadow all our blessing by complaining about what we don't have. If we begin to replace the time we spend complaining with counting our blessings, we will never be able to stop counting because God gives us new mercies every day.

BIBLICAL EXAMPLE OF GIVING THANKS- Paul is a great example of a person giving thanks to God in difficult situations. In Acts 16, Paul was thrown in jail for commanding an evil spirit to come out of a little girl. In jail, Paul did not throw himself a pity party instead he and Silas decided to rejoice in God. Acts 16:25 says, *"And at midnight Paul and Silas prayed and sang praises unto God."* Another incident of Paul giving God thanks will be found in 2 Corinthians 12:7-9. Paul had a thorn in his flesh. He went to God three times for God to remove it, and God responded to him *"My grace is sufficient for thee: for my strength is made perfect in weakness."* Instead of Paul becoming disappointed, he replied, *"Most gladly therefore will I rather glory in my* *infirmities that the power of Christ may rest upon me."* Although Paul knew the infirmity would remain, he chose to give thanks.

UTILIZE YOUR SPIRITUAL GIFTS- Hebrew 13:20-21 says, *"Now may the God of peace who brought up our Lord Jesus from the dead, the great Shepherd of the sheep, through the blood of the everlasting covenant make you complete in every good work to do his will, working in you what is well pleasing in his sight, to whom be glory forever and ever Amen."* This verse let us know the blood of Jesus made us complete. The completion was for us to do God's will. One way we can do God's will is to utilize our spiritual gift/gifts. God gave us spiritual gifts because it is his way of sharing His grace with others.

Exercising our gift allows us to be the hands and feet of Christ. Our gifts help edifies and build up the body of Christ. Make sure you are utilizing your gift. When we fail to utilize our gifts, we are walking in disobedience and we are out of the will of God. Failure to utilize our gift(s) cause the other members in the body to work harder and the body becomes dysfunctional.

Biblical examples of people utilizing their gift: In Nehemiah 8, Ezra used the gift of teaching to teach the people. In Luke 10, the Samaritan used the gift of mercy to help the man that was robbed, beaten, and left for dead. Priscilla and Aquilla used the gifts of help and allowed to Paul to live and work with them. Peter and John utilized the gift of healing in Acts 3 when they healed the man at the gate called Beautiful. Paul was constantly using the gift of exhortation through his letters to the church.

As believers, we must make sure we are utilizing our gift/gifts. Are you utilizing your gift? Do you know your gift? If you do not know your gift, seek God and ask him to reveal your gift to you. There are several resources out that can help us find our gifts and show us ways we can use our gift/gifts to edify the body of Christ. Use this resource as a guide https://gifts.churchgrowth.org/cgi-cg/gifts.cgi

Benefits of being in God's will (Psalm 91)

God's protection- Psalm 91:1-2- *He that dwelleth in the secret place of the most High* (God's Will) *shall abide under the shadow of the Almighty. I will say of the Lord, He is my refuge, and my fortress: my God; in him will I trust.*

God's deliverance- Psalm 91:3- *Surely, he shall deliver thee from the snare of the fowler, and from the noisome pestilence.* God will rescue us from every trap and protect us from fatal plagues.

A lack of fear- Psalm 91:5- *Thou shalt not be afraid for the terror by night; nor the arrow that flieth by day.* God will protect you from fear. Fear that comes from Satan. He will give you that power, love, and sound mind.

Destruction will be near, but it won't destroy you- Psalm 91:7-8- *A thousand shall fall at thy side, and ten thousand at thy right hand; but it shall not come nigh thee. 8. Only with thine eyes shalt thou behold and see the reward of the wicked.* Destruction will be near you, but it will not destroy you.

Remember Noah during the flood. The destruction was near him, all around him, but God protected him in that ark. He was in God's will. The Bible says Noah found grace in the eyes of God. Also, remember the children of Israel saw the Egyptian first born killed. Because they were in God's will by having that blood on their door post, their first born was not destroyed.

God will allow angels to protect us – Psalm 91:11- *For he shall give his angels charge over thee, to keep thee in all thy ways.*

God is not only going to protect us, but he is going to allow angels to protect us. We are double covered.

God will answer our call- Psalm 91:15- *He shall call upon me, and I will answer him: I will be with him in trouble, I will deliver him, and honour him.*

God will answer our call. Even if we have to wait a little while for the answer, just knowing He will answer gives us great confidence. This verse also lets us know that God is with us in trouble. God is with us during the good and He is with us when problems and situations arise in our lives. Many times, we forget God during the good (let us not forget him in good). We can call on God in the good for strength, joy, wisdom, etc.

God will give you long life- Psalm 91:16- *With long life will I satisfy him, and shew him my salvation.* God said, if you stay in my will, you will receive long life.

In conclusion, let us strive to get in the center of God's will. We know that we are in God's will when we are keeping his commandments. We know the only way we can keep God's commandments is to know them. The only way we can know His commandments is by reading His word.

I WANT TO BE IN HIS WILL

Day 29

I Can't Help the Way I am, But God Can

Roman 5:19- For as by one man's disobedience many were made sinners, so by the obedience of one shall many be made righteous.

This is just who I am. Have you ever said that phrase or have you ever heard anyone use that phrase? As believers, many times we don't fully use the scripture of 2 Corinthians 5:17, *Therefore if any man be in Christ, he is a new creature: old things are passed away; behold, all things are become new.*

The verse says all things are made new. That means that our personalities become new. We accept all the changes God wants to make until it comes to our personality. We love who we are, but God said I have made you a new creature. When we forget that God has made us new, we feel that we cannot help who we are. We feel that people should learn and adjust to our personality. The thing I can't help is coming into is this world a sinner.

Because Adam and Eve failed God, all of us were born sinners. Romans 5:12 states as by *one-man sin entered into the world, and death by sin; and so, death passed upon all men, for that all have sinned.* The good news is God sent us Jesus! Jesus can change who we are. Romans 5:19- *For as by one man's disobedience many were made sinners, so by the obedience of one shall many be made righteous.* What are some of the things we feel we can't help but to do:

- *I can't help but to gossip.*

- *I can't help but have low self-esteem.*

- *I can't help but worry.*

- *I can't help but complain.*

- *I can't help but be jealous.*

- *I can't help but procrastinate.*

- *I can't help but be bitter.*

- *I can't forgive them for the hurt they caused me.*

- *I can't make any time for God. My life is busy.*

In order for us to deal with our I can't attitude we must always keep in mind who Christ is:

According to Psalm 23- *He is our Shepherd*

According to Psalm 24- *The Earth belongs to Him*

According to Genesis 1- *He is the Creator*

According to Psalm 46:1- *He is our refuge and strength*

According to Psalm 27:1- *He is my light and my salvation*

According to Psalm 139- *He is all knowing, and he is everywhere*

According to Isaiah 6:1- *He is high and lifted up*

According to Jeremiah 32:27- *There is nothing too hard for him*

According to Matthew 19:26- *All things are possible with him*
There were characters in the Bible who faced I can't situation, but
God came in and changed their situation.

Woman with issue of blood- In Mark 5, we are introduced to the
lady who had an issue of blood. This lady couldn't get well. The Bible
tells us that the lady had her condition for 12 years. The Bible also
tells us that she went to different physicians. She spent all of her
money and she still did not receive healing. The lady heard about
Jesus, and she said to herself if I can just touch Him I will be heal.
The lady did just that. She touched Jesus, and that one touch made
her whole. Jesus was able to do what no doctor could do. Jesus was
able to heal this lady from a situation in which she couldn't help
herself.

The woman at the well- In John 4, we are introduced to the lady at
the well. This lady had a problem with men. She just could not say
no. Her problem was so bad that she had been married 5 times and
was now living with a boyfriend. Jesus offered this lady water which
would quench her thirst for men. He offered her living water that
would change her life. The lady was so free that she left all at the
well and went to tell others about this man name Jesus who told her
all things.

The man at the pool of Bethesda- In John 5, we meet the man at
the pool. He had an excuse for his situation. This man had been
dealing with his infirmity for 38 years. Jesus asked him a simple
question. The question was "Wilt thou be made whole?" That was a

yes or no question, but this man gave excuses of why he hadn't been heal. He told Jesus I have no one to put me in the water when the water is troubled. Jesus did not ask this man any more questions he told the man to rise take up his bed and walk, and the Bible says immediately the man was made whole. This man was in a situation in which he could not help himself, but Jesus came to his rescue and helped him out of his situation.

We must also keep in mind who we are in Christ. We must make daily affirmations of who we are in Christ over our lives. This will keep us from highlighting our I cant's. Every day say:

I am a conqueror- Romans 8:37- *Nay, in all these things we are more than conquerors through him that loved us.*

I am an overcomer- 1 John 4:4- *Ye are of God, little children, and have overcome them: because greater is he that is in you, then he that is in the world.*

I am victorious- 1 Corinthians 15:57- *But thanks be to God, which giveth us the victory through our Lord Jesus Christ.*

I am righteous- 2 Corinthians 5:21- *For he hath made him to be sin for us, who knew no sin; that we might be made the righteousness of God in him.*

I am fearfully and wonderfully made- Psalm 139:14

I am a chosen generation, a royal priesthood, a holy nation, a peculiar people. -1 Peter 2:9

In conclusion, we can't help how we came here, but we can help how we live here and where we go when we leave here. We have a Father Christ Jesus in whom we could put all our trust in and he is capable to guide us through this journey call life. His word tells us in Jude 24 now unto him that is able to keep you from falling, and to present you faultless before the presence of his glory with exceeding joy. It is a blessing knowing God can deliver us from the things we thought we couldn't help.

I CAN'T HELP WHO I AM, BUT GOD CAN

Haters are Builders

1 John 4:4- Ye are of God, little children, and have overcome them: because greater is he that is in you, than he that is in the world.

When people go around trying to tear you down or saying all matters of evil against you and about you, don't call them a hater just say they are building another step to my destiny. Look at the Bible character Joseph. You will find his story in Genesis 37-50. He had so many tear downs and evil done against him, but you never saw him call anyone a hater. You do see where it says the Lord was with him. Let's go through his story.

Joseph was first an outcast. His brothers did not like him because of favoritism shown to him by their father. He was next sold into slavery and was taken to a foreign land. After arriving in the foreign land, he became an overseer of his master's house until he became an object of lust to his master wife. When he rejected her, she lied on him which cause him to become a prisoner. Even in prison the Bible said the Lord was with him.

In prison, Joseph became in charge of all the prisoners. While in prison, God gave him the ability to interpret the dream of two other prisoners. Joseph told them the interpretation of their dreams and those things happened. Joseph asked the butler not to forget him when he is back working in his position. The butler did just that. He forgot Joseph for two years until the pharaoh had a dream. God used Joseph to interpret the dream which allowed Joseph to be elevated and honored. The only person over him was the pharaoh. Joseph's life was full of twists and turns and ups and downs, but he did not become bitter. There is nowhere in Joseph's story in which he gives a song of him weeping bitterly. He trusted the dream God showed him in Genesis 37. The dream of his brothers and parents bowing down to him. It took some time for the dream to manifest, but God manifested that dream. All his trials were a stepping stone to his destination.

Today, stop calling people haters. Stop worrying about who not supporting you. Don't worry about who is walking away. Trust the dream God has birthed in you. Remember just like God was right there with Joseph, he is right there with you. Do not complain another minute to anyone about what's going wrong. Just say thank you Lord for ordering my steps and for allowing others to build them.

Also, keep in mind that he prepares a table before you in the presence of your enemies. The same people who thought they were destroying you will one day be at the table God prepared for you. God going to allow you to feast with them because they did it for evil, but God did it for good. Work harder than you ever worked on your dream. You have the greatest supporter on your side. His name is God. He is El Shaddi. He is Jehovah. He is the all-knowing God.

DON'T DESPISE HATERS

www.ingramcontent.com/pod-product-compliance
Lightning Source LLC
LaVergne TN
LVHW051643080426
835511LV00016B/2459